P9-CME-421

1. Where Is God When You Need Him

WHERE IS GOD WHEN YOU NEED HIM?

WHERE IS GOD WHEN YOU NEED HIM?

Sharing Stories of Suffering with Job and Jesus: From Easy Answers to Hard Questions

Karl A. Schultz

Director Genesis Personal Development Center

ALBA · HOUSE   NEW · YORK

SOCIETY OF ST. PAUL, 2187 VICTORY BLVD., STATEN ISLAND, NY 10314

Scripture quotations are from The Revised Standard Version of the
Bible, copyright 1946, 1952, 1957 by the Division of Christian Education
of the National Council of the Churches of Christ in the United States of
America. Used with permission.

© 1992 by Karl A. Schultz

Library of Congress Cataloging-in-Publication Data

Schultz, Karl A., 1959 —
        Where is God when you need Him? : sharing stories of suffering
    with Job and Jesus : from easy answers to hard questions /
    by Karl A. Schultz.
            p.   cm.
        Includes bibliographical references.
        ISBN 0-8189-0623-5
        1. Suffering — Religious aspects — Christianity.
        2. Job (Biblical figure)   I. Title.
    BT732.7.S735   1992   91-35603
    231'.8 — dc20   CIP

Designed, printed and bound in the United States of
America by the Fathers and Brothers of the
Society of St. Paul, 2187 Victory Boulevard,
Staten Island, New York 10314, as part of their
communications apostolate.

© Copyright 1991 by the Society of St. Paul

PRINTING INFORMATION:

Current Printing - first digit   1 2 3 4 5 6 7 8 9 10 11 12

Year of Current Printing - first year shown
   1992   1993   1994   1995   1996   1997   1998   1999

DEDICATION

To
Jo-Ann, my wife and inspiration,
with Love

Acknowledgments

WITHOUT the encouragement, persistence, and faith of my wife, Jo-Ann, this book would never have seen the light of day. Her intuition and editorial insights proved decisive in shaping the manuscript into its final form. She made the project fun and fulfilling, as well as therapeutic. Thank God Job's wife and friends weren't as compassionate and understanding as Jo-Ann. Otherwise, we probably wouldn't have Job's wonderful prayer-laments as inspiration and consolation. Jo-Ann, thank you.

Contents

Contents

Introduction

THE QUESTION OF SUFFERING: NO EASY ANSWERS

THE WORLD is filled with easy answers, both religious and secular, to life's problems, chief of which is human suffering and its ultimate consummation, death. If we are having problems with our job, ministry, or family, there is no shortage of nice-sounding platitudes and confident advisors to help guide us. Their answers can skim the surface of most every form of psychological and spiritual suffering. So many theories about suffering exist that it is understandable if the modern sufferer or care-giver is overwhelmed by the choices. Of course, theories are fine until suffering visits *you*. Then, all answers seem to pale. All theories address the same nagging questions: What is the truth about suffering and divine justice? What perspective on suffering does justice to faith, reality, and my personal experience?

For Christians, the only satisfactory coping mechanism for suffering is faith in Jesus Christ. Jesus did not give an answer for suffering, but a way to live with it. His promises are more hopeful and realistic than the humanistic philosophers of our day, yet so often His liberating message is blunted. Part of our denseness is due to our aversion to the difficult questions He places before us. The stories of Job and Jesus are about human suffering and human possibilities. You won't find an ounce of propaganda or fluff in either story.

In *Where Is God When You Need Him?*, we will retell the story of Job in light of the story of Jesus and our own life story. Using a holistic, faith-story method, we will contemplate Job from a Christian personal growth perspective. We will explore how Job bears on everyday Christian actions and attitudes. We will also investigate a timeless Christian practice for experiencing God's word as personal, therapeutic, and transformational. Through the gift of *lectio divina*, each person is equipped to bring their feelings, questions, and experiences to God's word, and thereby not settle for second-hand answers.

Job is a natural starting point in any inquiry into suffering because his emotions and attitudes parallel ours. He is a model protester and pray-er for human sufferers. His values, virtues, and life vision are highly conducive to Christian growth and human development.

All suffering seems unjust or excessive in some way, and our tendency is to cry out, with the prophet Habakkuk, "Violence!"[1] It is only through the mysterious interaction of nature and grace that we can learn to repeat with Jesus, in response to the timeless temptation to enact revenge and retaliation, "Enough!"[2]

WHO THIS BOOK IS WRITTEN FOR

Where Is God When You Need Him? is designed for sufferers, care-givers, and individuals interested in personal growth. It does not assume familiarity with the book of Job, though it hopes to inspire enthusiasm for it. In our day, it may be particularly helpful to individuals who see themselves as Job figures in their job or vocation. Christians frequently fail to find support at the parish level when struggling with the day-to-day crosses of their employment or ministry. Many Christians turn to secular self-help and career counseling resources without considering the resources and wisdom available within their own faith tradition. Prayer, perseverance, trust in providence, and the ongoing discernment of one's vocation are Joban themes which are very relevant to modern vocational sufferers.

Where Is God When You Need Him? may have particular relevance to persons in the following groups:

Care-Givers

Job offers profound insights into the psycho-spirituality of suffering and care-giving. It dramatizes the coping language used by sufferers and care-givers. The progressive transformation of Job's life vision and consciousness reveals the stages sufferers typically pass through during the therapeutic process. Care-givers will find the positive and negative models of care-giving presented in Job particularly helpful for responding to troubled patients and families. Job is a colorful and instructive integration of spirituality, psychology, and the Kubler-Ross stages of death and dying.

Twelve-Step Program Participants And Care-Givers

Participants and care-givers in the various twelve-step programs will recognize the following values which play a central role in Job: reconciliation, honesty, integrity, humility, and the need for a higher power.

Persons Hurt By Religious Individuals And Institutions

Throughout history, religion has been used for both constructive and destructive purposes. In modern society, the suffering caused by religious individuals and institutions is highlighted and frequently exploited. However, such blaming does not remove the pain, and the hurt remains.

Job is a story that can accelerate the healing process in two ways. First, it portrays both the positive and negative aspects of religion in an objective, though exaggerated, manner. The author exposes the limitations of human wisdom and religious dogmas, and the damage that can result from an overzealous and insensitive application of these principles. He balances this with an example of an integrated religious person (Job) who remains faithful and virtuous amid tremendous suffering. Second, the story presents reconciliation and compassion as the constitutive elements of authentic religious practice. It challenges persons of all faiths to forgive those who have hurt them, no matter how deep the pain.

Persons critical of religion may find some of their deepest thoughts and emotions expressed eloquently and forcefully by Job. For those willing to ask hard questions of God, religion, and themselves, serious reflection on Job in the context of one's life experiences can be an opportunity for reconciliation with God, others, and life itself.

Persons Angry At God

Our modern age may psychoanalyze those who get angry or distressed with God, but the author of Job knows better. Properly channeled anger can stimulate personal growth and communication with God. We can best comprehend this anger by viewing it in the context of human relationships. Anger at God is similar to the anger we experience towards human beings we love, and on whom we place certain expectations. Anger is a sign that we care, and that some aspect or value of the relationship has been disturbed. It is a dynamic opportunity for a deeper understanding and relationship with God, neighbor, and ourselves. It holds great constructive and destructive potential, the fulfillment of which is dependent on the individual.

The book of Job gives the sufferer permission to express his or her deepest and darkest emotions to God. This can be an extremely cathartic and therapeutic experience. Keeping negative emotions and experiences bottled up within us is a ticket to health problems. Expressing them in a violent manner towards ourselves (e.g., substance abuse and suicide) or others (i.e., through acts of vengeance, bitterness, or withdrawal) is mentally, physically, and spiritually destructive. The reader will discover in Job a middle path that encourages the ventilation of negative experiences and emotions in a constructive manner while promoting hope in God's willingness to heal these in His own time.

THE BOOK OF SUFFERING

The Bible artfully avoids the extremes of nihilism (life is meaningless), rationalization (suffering can be explained), and spiritualization (religion or spirituality can provide simple answers to complex mysteries). It has not been called "the book of suffering" for nothing. As we will see, Job's problems start when he is afflicted "for nothing," and because he was good "for nothing."[3]

CHAPTER ONE

Job, Word Of God, And Healing

THE SIGNS OF THE TIMES

It is time to take the lanterns out from under our bushel baskets. Both western culture and the Church are in a severe crisis of values that is leading to a deterioration of society. An epidemic of mistrust, malaise, and hopelessness is sweeping society. Respect for human life and the environment continues to decline. Suffering and stress are clearly the primary negative signs of the times. They constitute a challenge for believer and non-believer alike.

While healing and transformation is necessary on a collective and individual basis, it has become clear that society is incapable of achieving this itself. Political, social, and economic efforts have largely failed to affect a reversal. The situation calls not for rhetoric, but for a radical revival of human values and virtues. Both secular culture and the Church have tried to facilitate reform and healing without repentance and holistic, long-term therapy. God's word, the therapy required by the situation, is no quick fix. Let us

consider how we can cooperate culturally with the divine
physician.

TOWARDS A CHRISTIAN CULTURE

We define Christian culture as a distinctly Christian way
of perceiving and responding to all facets of life. If we are to
be faithful to our Christian vocation, the Gospel must touch
all aspects of our life. Spiritual health, like physical health, is
holistic. Rather than a rejection of the world, Christian
culture works towards a Christianization of all that we
experience.

If we are serious about our faith, we inevitably ask
questions of the culture and environment we live in. Any
long-term therapy must treat both the individual and their
environment. Do our tastes in music, various forms of media
and entertainment, friends, art, hobbies, work, and literature build us and others up, or do they tempt and distract
us? Are they compatible with the values and principles revealed by God's word in Scripture, Tradition, and Church?

The transformation in attitude, awareness, and action
called for by these times need not make us austere, rigid, or
pharisaical. In its intimate familiarity with suffering, despair, prayer, hope, and the goodness of life, Job is the book
to inspire us to Christian culture and values. The word of
God is the mysterious healing agent necessary to effect the
transformation.

MORE THAN WORDS

When I speak of God's word or the word of God (used
interchangeably), I am referring to God's self-com-

munication, will, and saving action in human history. Although we encounter God's word primarily in Scripture, Christian Tradition, and the Living Church, God also reveals Himself in nature, persons, and in human events. The word of God cannot be confined or limited.

It is important to distinguish the Biblical concept of word from the modern concept. God's word in the sense of the Hebrew word *dabar* (pronounced da-var) and the Greek *logos* is a dynamic reality. For the ancients, *dabar* or *logos* was the holistic composite of word, thought, energy, and action. As powerful as the human word was, God's word was infinitely greater. In the timeless expression of the prophet Isaiah, God's word has power to achieve, and does not return to Him empty.[4]

GOD'S WORD AND THE CALL TO HUMAN INTEGRITY

God's word has an integrity or wholeness that is lacking in human words. Yet, God's word is vulnerable to human insincerity and self-seeking. As Job's friends demonstrate, it is difficult to witness to God's word when our word is not trustworthy. Job challenges us to cooperate with grace in disposing ourselves to be persons of integrity in whom God's word can dwell. The book of Job attests that suffering need not strip us of our integrity. We may temporarily lose hope and yield to sin out of weakness, but God has given us a spirit that is capable of cooperating with grace by regaining and maintaining our sense of dignity and integrity.

WHOLENESS VERSUS PERFECTION

God calls us to perfection in the Biblical sense of wholeness and integrity as creatures made in the image of God. What a motivation to self-esteem! What more profound tribute to God's goodness and humanity's dignity than to be made little lower than the angels (Psalm 8)!

These Biblical boosts to self-esteem enable me to affirm: I love myself because God does, and He's smarter than I am. Even when I don't want to like myself, my faith calls me not to give up. How can I love my neighbor if I don't love myself? This love of self is intrinsically tied to our status as creatures made in God's image. God thought enough of human beings to have His Son become one. If we wish to fulfill our human potential, or in Christian terms human vocation, who better to teach us how than Job and Jesus? They met suffering at its worst, were abandoned by human beings and seemingly by God, but still retained hope in God and themselves.

PRIORITIES AND PROCRASTINATION

Despite being aware of his sinfulness, St. Peter was willing to follow the Lord.[5] His sense of unworthiness didn't stop him. Will it stop us, or will we emulate his willingness to take up the challenge of God's call and word in the present moment? Is God's word enough of a treasure to distract us from our earthly pursuits? Are we waiting for that one decisive moment, that profound and grand call which may or may not come, or are we willing to start out by taking humble, small steps? Will we accept the insecurity and confusion that must accompany the joy and peace? If we are suffering, or caring for those in pain, can we devote ourselves to small, gradual steps in faith, hope, and love? This inglorious, painful path that we travel was also the road of Job.

It is time to follow Job's example in exchanging our weapons of retribution, rationalization, and rebellion for the sword of God's word. Because we will be working as wounded healers, we must immerse ourselves in the therapy that can accomplish God's will: God's word. Because God's word heals in conjunction with human therapy, we should first consider the prevalent values and perspectives of modern health-care.

HOLISTIC HEALTH-CARE IN THEORY AND PRACTICE

The therapeutic possibilities of medicine, psychotherapy, and pastoral care are universally recognized. A holistic (i.e. whole-person) approach to patient/client/parishioner care has been advocated since ancient times. In models of health-care and human development, the role of the human spirit and the importance of positive and balanced psycho-spiritual attitudes is well established. Researchers and practitioners constantly remind us of the link between the individual's health and their perspective on life. While the therapeutic nature of prayer, positive attitudes and images, faith, love, and hope, are almost universally accepted, the healing potential of God's word has received less attention, even within the Church. While it is clear in the lives of Job and Jesus that God's word has tremendous power to heal, all of us have trouble making the transition from theory to practice. Most of our difficulties can be attributed to human weakness and the skepticism and secularization of our times.

The process of applying God's word is itself very vulnerable. It is subject to all sorts of abuses, oversights, and errors in discernment and application. There is no blueprint telling us how to discern, interpret, and respond to God's word. We are not guaranteed infallibility, even if we possess a listening heart, humble spirit, and pliant will.

The beginning chapters in Exodus which chronicle the liberation of Israel are an excellent paradigm of the quandary human beings find themselves in: How to integrate faith in God's word and power with responsible human action. Nowhere is this more dramatically illustrated than in Ex 14:13-15, where a call to trust in God's word is immediately followed by an exhortation to human action: "But Moses said to the people, 'Do not be afraid, stand firm, and see the deliverance that the LORD will accomplish for you today; for the Egyptians whom you see today you shall never see again. The LORD will fight for you, and you have only to keep still.' Then the LORD said to Moses, 'Why do you cry out to me? Tell the Israelites to go forward.' "

For Christians, God's word is an essential complement to medical and psychotherapeutic efforts at healing. It is the spiritual catalyst of holistic health, which in our times has been compartmentalized into (for purposes of discussion rather than reality, as the human person is more properly seen as a mysterious whole than as a sum of diverse parts) mind, body, and spirit components. Too often Christians uncritically derive their perspective and values on issues such as self-esteem, success, fasting, suffering, sexuality, life necessities, stress management, and time management from secular sources. Secular resources and wisdom have their place in the formation of the human psyche and spirit, but they must be imbued with the values of the word of God as revealed in Scripture, Tradition, and the living Christian Community.

WORD OF GOD AND LIFE VISION

To bring us to the level of practicality, I would like to focus on the word of God as it relates to the individual's basic outlook on life. The Christian approach to life fundamentally differs from that of the personal growth and human potential movement. Both Christianity and secular humanism promote themselves as offering truth, happiness, growth, and healing. While there have been numerous attempts to reconcile the two, there exists a fundamental difference in orientation from which all other differences flow.

At the heart of the Christian message is the paschal mystery, the suffering, death, and resurrection of Jesus, and the Incarnation. These realities are to be experienced in an intimate and practical way by Jesus' followers. They serve as a moral and spiritual foundation for discernment and decision-making, ethics, human relationships, and vocational activities. One objective of our study of Job is to suggest some practical applications of the paschal and incarnational wisdom of Job.

While secular humanism extols legitimate human values such as self-actualization, self-knowledge, and unconditional love, it does not acknowledge the centrality of the cross, the omnipresence of God, redemptive suffering, and the hereafter. While Christians try to balance their attention between earthly and heavenly concerns, secular philosophies are by definition preoccupied with earthly matters. Given the contradictory stances of secular humanism and Christianity, the values, decisions, attitudes, and actions which emanate from these belief systems are bound to be different. As we work through Job, we will highlight issues and situations where their cross purposes and contradictory values are apparent.

The book of Job is an excellent place to begin speaking of God's word as therapy, for it concerns itself with suffering, religion, and the meaning and fundamental vocation of human existence. In Job, the interrelationship of holistic health, psycho-spiritual growth, and religious truth is dramatized in practical fashion. In light of the vast cultural differences between Job's time and ours, practical instruction in the art of interpreting and responding to God's word communicated in human words is necessary. How can we dispose ourselves to be recipients, sharers, and instruments of God's healing word?

LECTIO DIVINA: *A HOLISTIC PATH TO GOD, GROWTH, AND HEALING*

Within the Christian tradition there is a simple, proven model for assimilating God's word into our hearts. *Lectio divina*[6] is a therapeutic and transformational path for believers to encounter God and His will in the word of God. The thought-provoking, open-ended nature of Job is particularly amenable to *lectio divina*.

While *lectio divina* has traditionally been confined to spiritual reading, its framework can also serve as a path to God's presence and values in the Eucharist, human encounters and relationships, nature, and the daily events of life. Because God's word and involvement cannot be confined, neither should we rigidly confine our *lectio divina*. The original purpose of *lectio divina* in the monastic setting was to enable the monk to communicate with God and listen to His word. While we ought to start with and concentrate on the Bible, and perhaps eventually progress to works which are in effect a commentary on or application of Biblical truths,[7] we need not limit ourselves to these entities. God can reveal

Himself in many ways and places. The Bible itself, and in particular the book of Job, leads us to discover God's presence and imprint on all things.

Lectio divina is a framework and guide in our efforts to experience God's word, presence, and silence in both commonplace and extraordinary human affairs, starting with our discernment of His activity in our own life. In the next chapter, we will sketch out the basics of *lectio divina* and refer the reader to resources for digging more deeply into its riches.

CHAPTER TWO

Lectio Divina: Framework

Lectio divina describes the holistic (i.e. whole person: mind, body, and spirit) progression through which the Christian encounters God in the Scriptures. Although often defined as a method, it is more appropriately termed a process. Bible readers unfamiliar with the tradition of *lectio divina* commonly pass through its stages as a natural progression of their prayer and reflection. Its simplicity and facilitation of heart-felt communication with God make it ideal for persons experiencing suffering and stress.

Lectio divina dates to the fourth century A.D., and is preceded by methods and principles of biblical interpretation used in the rabbinic schools. The English translation of the Latin *lectio divina*, divine reading or listening, implies that we are engaging in an inspired activity. It is both an active and receptive process: We use our imagination, intuition, and analytical skills as best we can (nature), and wait for God to respond as He sees fit (grace).

Lectio divina is composed of four interactive and progressive movements that lead us toward an encounter with

- 11 -

God. Although we distinguish between them for purposes of discussion, in practice they are sufficiently interwoven and interdependent that rigid distinctions are somewhat artificial. The mysterious, graced flow which characterizes our praying of Scripture is not conducive to precise analysis. In *lectio divina*, the means is entirely directed towards the end, communion with God. The process is designed to be natural and uplifting rather than mechanical and burdensome. Each person must adapt *lectio divina* to their abilities and circumstances.

The following will serve as a basic guide to *lectio divina*. Each stage is introduced with its traditional Latin name followed by the English translation. It is highly recommended that readers who choose to utilize this framework in their daily devotions consult the resources discussed at the conclusion of this chapter.

LECTIO: *READING*

- Slowly read and reread a brief passage of Scripture.

- If possible, read the passage aloud, or at least mouth or whisper the words. This fuller involvement of the senses contributes to the holistic quality of prayer. In former times, monks listened to the text as much through the voice and ears as with the eyes. We speak, hear, see, and (by gently holding the Bible, perhaps even following the words with our finger to slow us down) touch the word. Medieval monastic practitioners spoke of figuratively tasting the words through slow, meditative recitation.

- Slow, vocal reading of Scripture can induce a certain rhythm into prayer. Gentle recitation and repetition of words can slow our breathing down and relax us.

- Ask questions of the text. What is its context? What has happened in the book up to now? We may want to skim the previous passage or chapter in order to situate the text. How might its literary form — i.e., history, parable, proverb, moral exhortation, lament, story, analogy, hymn, etc. — influence your interpretation? What seems to be the purpose of the speaker or narrator: i.e., corrective, affirming, exhortation, denunciation, warning, explanatory, informational, etc.? What images does the passage evoke? Are there any repetitive or similar nouns, verbs, or phrases that hint of its general theme or meaning?

- During our reading, a particular thought, theme, image, or verse may strike a chord within us. If so, we should linger over it and try to discern why this speaks to us. With practice, we will develop the ability to intuit when to continue with our reading and when to remain with the provocative text, perhaps for the entire period of our quiet time.

MEDITATIO: *MEDITATION*

- Synthesize the individual thoughts, themes, and morals of the passage. Balance analysis of the individual parts with a consideration of the passage as a whole. Try to deduce an overall meaning or message. What is the central teaching or moral? What values and principles is the passage promoting? Is there a particular meaning or message in either the individual parts or the passage as a whole that God seems to be placing before us? What truths about God, human beings, and human existence are being revealed? What truths about ourselves or our current situation does the text touch upon? How does this passage touch our personal experience and emotions? To what attitudes or actions are we being called?

- Memorization: Some individuals find that selecting small chunks of Scripture for memorization is helpful for internalizing the message. The original monastic practice of *meditatio* involved the memorization of the text for the purpose of ingraining God's word into one's being. In this we notice parallels with the personal growth practices of affirmations and visualizations. Providing we approach the practice with Christian goals and values, we have precedents for using Scripture texts as personal affirmations or auto-suggestions to be repeated several times on a periodic basis. While the monks didn't use terms such as affirmation or auto-suggestion, and were not acquainted with the subconscious mind as we know it, they were quite cognizant of the need to be holistically transformed by Scripture. They understood perhaps better than we do the importance of having God's word penetrate our being.

- The rich imagery of Scripture is also well-suited for the practice of visualization. The ancient writers wrote to impress certain images on the minds of their audience. In the context of *lectio divina*, visualization is simply appropriating the images conveyed by Scripture into our conscious and subconscious mind. It is not a question of making the image an idol or an end in itself. Rather, it is to replace destructive images which exist in our consciousness with positive images from Scripture. The most obvious image for appropriation is that of the crucified Christ. For example, we can recall and affirm this image when we are tempted to be retaliatory and unforgiving. Scientists tell us that the human mind subconsciously converts words into images which can deeply affect our behavior. We think in pictures rather than words. If the Gospel is to transform our whole selves, this must include our internal images as well. We use visualization to root ourselves more deeply in God's word, rather than to gain power, possessions, and prestige. We can sharply distinguish such visualization from popular subliminal methods which are not God-centered or self-directed and therefore impose on us the value systems of those who compose the inaudible message.

- The objective of personal affirmations and visualizations in a Christian context is to ingrain the truths of God's word into our conscious and subconscious mind. We wish to replace unhealthy and destructive attitudes, images, and beliefs with positive ones steeped in Christian truths. The Bible is an excellent resource for building up self-esteem, self-discipline, unconditional love, and sincere respect for others through the use of affirmations and visualizations.

ORATIO: *PRAYER*

- We express to God our heartfelt response to this passage. In what tone, words, and message does this passage inspire us to communicate with God? Our response can take many forms: praise, thanksgiving, silence, lament, questioning, anger, petition, etc. The Benedictine spiritual direction adage applies: Pray as you can, not as you can't.

- The expression of our thoughts and feelings to God need not stay within the confines of the passage we are reflecting upon. Our reflection on the text may be a catalyst to communicate some heartfelt message to God that is unrelated to the text. Initially, we should try to be faithful to the scriptural passage on which we are meditating. When unrelated concerns and emotions come to the fore, deal with them and eventually return to the text. If such distractions become habitual, they should be handled outside of *lectio divina*, whether through prayer, reflection, or as part of therapy or spiritual direction.

- Ideally, *oratio* should involve us physically as well as spiritually and mentally. If we are praising God, we can make some worshipping gesture with our bodies. If we are angry with God, we can express this physically, perhaps with a clenched fist. If we wish to ask something of God, we might involve our hands, arms, and voice.

- Hey, wait a minute. Did you say anger? Anger in prayer, a contradiction in terms, an invitation to divine retribution? Are you nuts? Are you prescribing a violation of the ten commandments? Holy persons don't get angry at God, do they?

- Why have our religious tradition and western culture relegated unpleasant feelings such as anger and resentment to the periphery of prayer and religious expression, as if they exist only as aberrations? The Scriptures clearly reveal that healthy human relationships do not exclude anger. Most of the biblical characters presented to us as models of holiness experience and display anger towards someone they love, including God. Thank God for Job, Jeremiah, the Psalms, the Prophets, and Jewish tradition for dramatically acknowledging and praying these feelings.

- The Scripture text itself, especially biblical prayers such as the Psalms, can serve as our prayer. Praying the words of Scripture aloud or mouthing them quietly can move us from the head to the heart. We need not scrupulously adhere to the literal content of Scripture. Sometimes responding to scriptural inspiration in our own words, images, and feelings makes our prayer more heartfelt. The contrast between head and heart dialogue is dramatically illustrated by the dialogue between Job's friends (speaking from the head) and Job (proceeding from the heart.)

- Scriptural messages that are hard for us to swallow are especially fruitful subjects for prayer, providing we honestly acknowledge our indigestion before God — just as we would share our disapproval with a dear friend. We may experience a certain dryness, frustration, or emotional discomfort with the text, but such difficulties with

Scripture often reveal areas in need of growth or healing. It is human nature to expose only our health to the divine doctor. Yet, it is the wounds that most interest Him.[8]

CONTEMPLATIO: *CONTEMPLATION*

- *Contemplatio* constitutes a natural progression from active prayer (*oratio*) to receptive prayer. Our listening faculties are especially prominent in this stage. We wait for the Lord by allowing Him time to respond to our prayer. We commit ourselves to being rather than doing for the Lord. This being disposes us for the doing when the time for action arrives. Those with busy schedules take note: A common side-effect of setting aside quiet times on a daily basis is an increase in efficiency and purposefulness.

- If we submit to the temptations of our hyperactive, noisy culture, and skip *contemplatio*, we will be posing questions and petitions to God without listening for His response!

- Many of us have trouble sitting still, even for a few moments. If so, *contemplatio* will require practice, self-discipline, and patience. If we can discipline ourselves to slow down and be quiet, if only for a few moments, the Holy Spirit can deepen our prayer experience and gift us with a greater awareness of God's presence in our daily activities. The awareness and devotional exercises of Fr. Anthony de Mello, S.J. contained in *Sadhana: A Way to God: Christian Exercises in Eastern Form* have proven to be an excellent stimulant of both relaxation and contemplation for many individuals.

- *Centering Prayer* is a Christian method for facilitating contemplation that can be used during this stage. It is designed to help persons become aware of, in rhythm with, and responsive to God's presence through the gentle repetition of a simple word or phrase. This word or phrase also helps us cope with distractions. See the bibliography for recommended resources.

- However we pursue contemplation, the common denominator is always silence, simple presence, humility, and receptivity.

- As discussed in chapter ten, Job provides a balanced and earthy model for contemplation. He anticipates the mystical tradition of the Church.

CHAPTER THREE

Lectio Divina:
Practical Considerations

USING LECTIO DIVINA *WITH JOB*

The following suggestions for using *lectio divina* with Job are based on my experience in Bible studies, Schools of the Word,[9] support groups, and in presenting "*Job Therapy*" programs to pastoral care-givers and health-care professionals.

Quality Versus Quantity: A Little Job Can Go A Long Way

The sheer size of the book of Job should caution us against biting off too much text at one time. Because of the cultural distance which we must travel in order to understand the book, it is likely that there will be verses and sections that completely elude us. The art of *lectio divina* is to be sensitive both to the Holy Spirit and to our own abilities,

limitations, experiences, and needs. It is best to concentrate
on those verses and chapters that speak to us as opposed to
beating our heads against the wall on texts which leave us
high and dry.

One verse of Job may be enough to spark meditation,
prayer, and contemplation. Job is filled with pregnant
phrases and colorful images that can touch upon our emotions and experiences. This is true on a practical as well as
spiritual level. For example, in Job 7:19, Job asks God when
He will let him alone long enough to swallow his spit. This
may remind us of times when we felt like life was closing in
on us and we didn't have time to breathe, let alone function
properly. Job 7:4 and 7:13-15 describe Job's inability to find
rest at night, an experience familiar to persons suffering ill
health. We can take these and other verses and pray them in
light of our experiences, perhaps transposing them into our
own words and circumstances. By repeating them softly and
pondering them in our hearts, we give the message time to
sink deep into our consciousness. It is important to follow
this with prayer and contemplation, so that we balance our
own interpretation, reaction, and desires with God's healing
presence and wisdom.

Suggested Reading Progression

If we are unfamiliar with Job, it is wise to consult an
outline of the book and an introductory article providing
background information. We might also skim the book to
get an overview of the story. For purposes of *lectio divina*, it is
usually best to begin with the less overtly theological sections
of Job. This would include the prologue (chapters 1 and 2),
the epilogue (42:7-17), and Job's laments (chapters 3-31)
and acceptance speech (42:1-6). We could also tackle the

Yahweh Speeches (chapters 38-41) and the Wisdom Poem (chapter 28), if only to appreciate their beautiful poetry and practical philosophy. They are a high point of one of the most compelling aspects of Job, its nature-inspired theological insight.

The speeches of Job are easier for sufferers to relate to than the speeches of his friends. The friends' speeches are best approached last, especially by sufferers, for they sound too much like the rational and religious answers we frequently hear in response to our troubles. Unlike Job, whose speeches reveal a gradual expansion of consciousness and increase in intensity, the friends' speeches progress primarily in vehemence rather than in insight. They seem content to recycle and reword their arguments, rather than reflect upon and refine them. Familiarity with the cultural background and theological themes underlying their speeches is helpful for understanding them on a deeper level.

Care-givers can read the friends' speeches with profit by using them as a mirror and check-point for detecting how their own response to sufferers parallels the friends'.

Taking The High With The Dry

Because God often seems remote during times of suffering and stress (almost as if He were testing us!), it is important that we let go of any competitive or scrupulous tendencies when we practice *lectio divina*. Remember, we are doing this primarily out of obedience to God. He's in charge, we're only His servants. What is important is that we use our abilities as best we can while remaining open to both divine and human correction. If we allocate sufficient time for *lectio divina*[10] and our experience is dry, we need to let go of our disappointment and move on. According to prayer authorities such as St. John of the Cross, St. Teresa of Avila, and Fr. J.P. de Caussade,[11] a dry prayer period accepted obediently can do us more good than one in which we receive various consolations and insights.

Job, A Lectio Divina *Person Himself*

I do not think we would be 'proof texting' or projecting a thematic bias into Job if we posited that he went through the stages of *lectio divina* in preparation for meeting God. Instead of discovering God's word and initiative in Scripture, he discovered it in his present painful circumstances. His 'concluding arguments' in chapters 29-31 are essentially a public examination of conscience which he could only have attained through interior awareness, meditation, and prayer. Throughout his earlier speeches, he made frequent references to Scripture as it bore on his current situation. The *lectio-meditatio* stage of Job's reflection consists of his contrasting of Scripture texts from memory with his current experience of life. Part of the function of *lectio divina* is to so ingrain God's word into our being that we naturally recall it at critical points in our life.

Perhaps the most profound example of such scriptural internalization and application is the passion of Jesus. All four evangelists interpret the dark events in the light of the Scriptures, especially the Psalms. In fact, the final words on Jesus' lips as reported by Matthew, Mark, and Luke are recitations of Ps 22:2 and Ps 31:6. At the pivotal moment of His life, the Word Himself used the word of God to express what He was experiencing. In Jesus, Job, and later St. Stephen, the first Christian martyr,[12] we have quite a precedent for making the words of Scripture our own when we are put to the test.

It is much easier to digest the Yahweh Speeches if we approach them contemplatively. Taken literally, God's response to Job is hardly gentle and compassionate. Further, it is remote from our experience. Few of us expect to be confronted so directly by God. Through contemplation, the same message conveyed to Job could be communicated by the Holy Spirit in each of our hearts. For example, practically each verse of chapters 38-39 highlights an element of nature that is suitable for contemplation of the mysteries of creation and providence.

If we assume that Job participated in the divine revelation through contemplation, it is easier to understand why he was so transformed by it. When considered as the fruits of contemplation, the message becomes more personal and less intimidating. God invites us, like Job, to experience life from His perspective through the vehicle of contemplation. This contemplation is not consigned only to quiet, meditative settings. As the writings of St. Teresa of Avila remind us, we can experience God's presence and call in our daily work and interactions as naturally as during our prayer time. If Job encountered God through contemplation, there is certainly hope and opportunity for us!

Working Through Job And Suffering In Community

The intense and provocative nature of both Job and human suffering make a support group environment an ideal setting for *lectio divina*. It is much easier to stick with Job when you are working through it with others, especially under the direction of a trained guide. The sheer length, wordiness, and the time-conditioned nature of the book may make it prohibitive for persons unacquainted with Scripture. Its thematic richness and theological subtlety is much more discernible through the 'brainstorming' effect of shared Scripture reading. Perhaps most important, a support group gives people a forum for sharing the questions, insights, and emotions evoked by the text in the context of their life experiences.

The Transformational Values Of Job

The use of *lectio divina* with Job can make an impression both on the conscious and unconscious level.

On the conscious level, Job impresses on us the importance of personal integrity and respect for others. He doesn't rationalize shortcuts in the areas of sexual, business, and social morality.[13] He inspires us to treat others in business, social, and familial interactions the way we would wish to be treated. As we contrast Job's values with our own and society's, we become aware of areas of personal justice in which we need to grow. Unlike modern society, Job defined success in terms of integrity and dignity rather than results and usefulness.

On the subconscious level, Job exemplifies the staying power of a clean conscience. While he realizes he could be wrong, he sincerely believes he's innocent, and that's enough for him to refute his human accusers and persist in his plea of innocence. Job is a model of determination that is quite timely in our age of skepticism, pessimism, and fear of risk and commitment. He bases his self-image on divine values flowing from his origin and destination in God. Without such a strong foundation, he could not have withstood the barrage of rational arguments and religious accusations from his would-be comforters.

Seeking God With Job

The question "Where is God when I need Him?" underlies much of Job's laments. For example, Job 23:8-9: "But if I go to the east, he is not there; or to the west, I cannot perceive him; where the north enfolds him, I behold him not; by the south he is veiled, and I see him not." In chapter 24, he voices this question on behalf of the universal community of sufferers, his protest reaching a zenith in 24:12: "From the dust the dying groan, and the souls of the wounded cry out (yet God does not treat it as unseemly)." By reflecting on some of Job's unorthodox accusations of God, we can get more in touch with our own rebellion and lack of peace. We can balance this with the divine perspective as revealed in the Wisdom Poem, Yahweh Speeches, Job's acceptance speech, and epilogue.

CHOOSING A TEXT

If we wish to practice *lectio divina* on texts other than Job, there are a variety of approaches one can take. We can do a thematic study as presented in Thelma Hall's *Too Deep for Words: Rediscovering Lectio Divina*, or we can work our way through one of the biblical books, or follow the Church's cycle of daily readings. It is often helpful to begin *lectio divina* with a Psalm or a portion thereof that describes one's current mood. Each person must choose the format that works best for them. For further discussion of the various options, consult one of the popular introductory guides on Scripture reading listed in the bibliography.

USE OF A COMMENTARY

If we wish to consult a commentary or the textual footnotes found in most Bibles, we should do so either during or prior to *lectio* (to provide us with a background for reading the passage) or during *meditatio* (to shed light on confusing, obscure passages). The problem with consulting a commentary amid our *lectio divina* is that we may get side-tracked from the task at hand. Reading a commentary may be a tempting alternative to confronting ourselves and God's word. Unless we are dealing with a particularly laborious or confusing text, it is usually better to read and meditate on the passage prior to consulting a commentary. This enables us to come fresh to the passage, and perhaps learn something about ourselves from our initial reaction to the text. We can always consult a commentary as a follow-up to our *lectio divina*.

Familiarity with a text through prior reading, commentaries, sermons, or classroom instruction is a gift that enables us to avoid reinventing the wheel. Familiarity becomes a hindrance only when we lazily settle for previous interpretations and applications. Each time we read Scripture, we should broaden, deepen, and challenge our previous understanding.

PERSONAL LETTERS FROM GOD

God invites both individual and community to discover meaning and guidance in their suffering through a personal encounter with Him in the words, persons, and events of the Bible. The Bible becomes relevant for us when we recognize that we are the characters, and ours are the values and choices that the word of God confronts. Scripture is unlike any other literary work in that it is profoundly personal in nature. The inspiration of the Holy Spirit makes this possible. We would do well to keep in mind the words of St. Gregory the Great, himself a profound yet practical commentator on the book of Job: "What is Sacred Scripture if not a letter from God to his creature? If you were to find yourself away from headquarters, posted in some distant place and you received a letter from your earthly emperor you would not be at ease, you would not go to rest or have a nap until you found out what your emperor had to say to you. The emperor of the heavens, the Lord of the angels and of humankind has sent you his letters. They have a bearing on your very life and yet, my son, you show no anxiety to read these letters! Get down to it, I implore you, and find a way to meditate daily on the words of your creator. Learn to know the mind of God in the Word of God" (taken from Gregory's letter to Theodorus, personal physician to the Emperor).

KEEPING A PERSONAL OR LECTIO DIVINA *JOURNAL*

If Scripture is a personal letter from God, it is only natural that we may wish to respond with a letter of our own. The challenging and stimulating words of Scripture and the similar nature of life make journal keeping (a structured form of letter writing) a natural companion to *lectio divina*. Sometimes we need a vehicle of communication where we will not be second-guessed, criticized, or interrupted. We need to get our difficult emotions out of our system, both to understand them and as a form of prayer. A journal can help us get to the root of our feelings, especially during times of suffering and stress. Writing our thoughts down brings objectivity into the interpretation process; our thoughts and feelings acquire a certain independence that is easier for us to analyze. In addition, some people find it easier to express their innermost thoughts at the point of a pen.

A journal kept during stressful times could be referred to as a Job Journal. Our journal can enable us, like Job, to ventilate our emotions in a constructive manner. The speeches of Job are refined dramatizations of a sufferer's journal. We can use images, verses, and passages of Job as an inspiration or catalyst to our journal writing. Such ventilation can lead to self-discovery, discernment, and a greater awakening of our potential.[14] The list of journal keepers in the Christian tradition is impressive, including such luminaries as Dag Hammarskjold, St. Augustine, Thomas Merton, St. Therese of Lisieux, and Pope John XXIII, to name a few.

We can use a journal as a diary to record events and feelings, or as a spiritual journal to discuss our perception of God's initiative and our response during the day. We usually end up with some combination of the two. While journal keeping need not be complicated, I recommend that the beginner consult a basic text on journal-keeping. Refer to the bibliography for recommended texts.

A *lectio divina* journal is simply a compilation of Scripture texts that speak to us. They may or may not be annotated by our personal comments and reflections. Unlike a personal journal, which most people use on a daily or consistent basis, a *lectio divina* journal can be used more loosely. *Lectio divina* of itself requires a considerable amount of discipline. A *lectio divina* journal should be motivational and inspirational in nature. Making it a compulsive activity might turn us off to *lectio divina* altogether.

There will be times when our *lectio divina* will seem

uninspired to us, and nothing within the Bible passage particularly moves us. Or, we may wish to spend our time on the emotions and experiences which the biblical passage evokes. At other times there will be passages which strike a chord in us, and we wish to single out for future reference. Whether we record these emotions and experiences or the scriptural text itself in either our personal or *lectio divina* journal is a matter of personal choice.

Recording Scripture words or texts that touch us can be a memory aid. If we want to internalize a particular message, we can consult our journal periodically to provide the reinforcement necessary to ingrain the passage in our memory and subconscious. Writing the text down of itself helps to imprint the text on our mind. One practical advantage of the *lectio divina* journal is that it helps us keep our Bibles somewhat tidy. While underlining or highlighting texts and writing brief notes in our Bible is highly recommended, copious notes or underlined passages create clutter that makes future reading more difficult. This clutter can motivate us to rely on previous interpretations instead of exploring how the text speaks to me today.

When I choose to use a journal in conjunction with *lectio divina*, I simply date the journal page and begin writing. I find single-spacing the individual text and double-spacing between texts or personal reflections to be the most readable format. Periodically, I will refer to the journal and perhaps repeat softly a particular passage that I find relevant to my current disposition and situation. If I make the journal too structured or laborious, especially during "hard times," I'll lack the energy to maintain it. The simpler the better.

Writing in either a personal or *lectio divina* journal can of itself be a form of prayer. It can also lead to other forms of prayer, such as vocal prayer (praying aloud) or silent mental prayer. A journal can be an excellent vehicle for bypassing the superficial niceties which so often mark our prayer en route to an honest sharing of deep feelings, thoughts, and beliefs.

A journal, like *lectio divina*, is an instrument for growth and healing. The manner in which we conduct these activities should be determined by what helps us grow and heal. Too much or too little discipline or structure can either discourage or fail to challenge us. Prayer, practice, and experimentation can help us find the right combination and balance.

ACCENTUATING THE HUMAN

The most common mistake made by beginners in practicing *lectio divina* is the imposition of an exaggerated piety or supernatural bias into the interpretation process. We need to permit the biblical characters, including Jesus, to be human. Otherwise we might excuse ourselves from deep involvement in the text by rationalizing that they were of a different mettle, or in a different situation. Such rationalization blunts the impact and practical application of the passage. An overly reverential reading of Scripture detaches its persons, circumstances, and events from real life and our common experience.

Accentuating the human also entails recognizing the human author's objectives in the biblical text. Anyone who takes *lectio divina* seriously will want to acquire at least an elementary awareness of the historical context of the Bible, as well as a basic grasp of biblical study principles developed by the Church for interpreting and applying a scriptural text. We would be wise in following the traditional middle path of the Church which gives consideration to both the human and divine influence in the text. These are obviously not readily differentiated, and therefore must be held in a constructive tension. The difficulty in keeping these in balance is one reason *lectio divina* is especially appropriate in a group setting as a supplement to our private devotions.

WORD IN COMMUNITY

It is important to be realistic about the practice of *lectio divina*. Individuals will be drawn to it in different ways and degrees. Some persons may be more comfortable going through the *lectio divina* steps in contemplation of a newborn baby, an afflicted person loving their family, a sunset, the ocean, or a recent or past event in their life. *Lectio divina* is a gift that God gives in a myriad of ways. While it is most appropriate for Scripture and other spiritual reading, it is worth emphasizing that it should not be used to put God or religious practice in a straitjacket.

Through pastoral experience, I have found that people need varying amounts of structure and time in their *lectio divina*. Some people do *lectio divina* best in a group. It is very difficult for them to practice by themselves. These same people may be capable of sitting for hours in contemplation of nature, while those more comfortable with Scripture may not perceive God as readily in nature or in daily events. For those uncomfortable with Scripture, a simple five minute period focusing on just one or two verses seems to work best. For those naturally drawn to Scripture, more time and text are necessary.

The point is that we need each other. Our gifts need to be shared so they can build up each other and the community. What I lack, another can supply. This is one of the principles underlying the success of support groups in the secular world. Sharing of each other's burdens is a natural fit for the Christian community.

Because *lectio divina* involves the whole self, it requires a commitment of time and energy. A group environment helps in the area of discipline, structure, and background knowledge, as well as in the practice of shared silence. Without the structure of *lectio divina*, or a derivative framework of some sort, group Bible studies can become opinion forays where everyone stays pretty much at the level of the head. It is much more difficult to get off-track when you are delving into Scripture at the level of the senses, personal experience, and the heart, than when you are simply discussing opinions. Each person needs to strive for practicality in their response to Scripture: How will the word of God make a difference in my life in the present moment and circumstance?

Even a few minutes of silence can unleash the Spirit and transform a Bible study. When we contemplate together, and noise no longer separates us, it becomes more apparent that we are sisters and brothers, and that the Bible and prayer are not to be detached from daily life. *Lectio divina* helps people slow down together, get into a personal and collective rhythm, and leave the hustle-bustle of their individual worlds to sit for a few moments at the Lord's feet, surrounded by His family.

The efficacy of group contemplation of Scripture was noted long ago by St. Gregory the Great: "I know from experience that frequently in the company of my brothers I have understood many things about the Word of God that on my own I did not succeed in understanding. It is you who enable me to learn what I teach. This is the truth; rather often I tell you that which I hear when I am with you."[15]

LECTIO DIVINA, *SUFFERING, AND PERSONAL GROWTH*

Lectio divina is ideal for sufferers and care-givers because of its simplicity, flexibility, and practicality. When we are hurting or angry at the deepest level of our being, we will not be satisfied with indirect communications or second hand answers. We want to go to the source of our anger. *Lectio divina* does not guarantee that we will get answers, or that we will find a cure for our problems. It does dispose us, however, to hear and accept God's word. From a worldly perspective, practicing *lectio divina* during times of suffering is foolish. The broken world we live in encourages us to imitate Job's wife and fall into despair. The world offers many ways for us to give up, cop out, and run away. Conversely, Job exhorts us to persevere in our faith and integrity.

Presumably, Job's tolerance of suffering is no greater than anyone else's. He hounds God for what he perceives as God's hounding of him. Job can inspire us to continue to hope in God, and cling to our values, even when it seems to be "for nothing."[16] He teaches us that anger at God and love for Him can co-exist in the suffering believer. To internalize this insight to the fullest extent, we need to move gradually through reading/listening, meditation, prayer, and contemplation. The word of God then becomes a mirror for us; it exposes our fears, weaknesses, and hurts, as well as our hopes and strengths. If we persist in our efforts, we will bear the fruit of reconciliation, thus making our suffering redemptive and allying it with the Lord's.

It is interesting that many proponents of personal growth programs and resources make grander claims for their system than the Bible does for itself.[17] This despite the fact that the authority behind the Bible is both God and the

Church, while personal growth programs are based solely on human testimony. The word of God makes its promises conditional to both humanity's and God's free response. The Bible freely acknowledges and confronts the problems, disappointments, and tragedies of life. The promises given to Christians by the word of God speak to our faith rather than our self-centeredness. The word of God calls us to a life of trust and earthly insecurity. As Job discovered, personal righteousness, providence, and divine justice do not guarantee us smooth sailing. When our seas become rough, *lectio divina* is a path for communicating our pain to God, and asking for His help and guidance.

If we are going to practice *lectio divina*, it is important that we recognize that it is not inferior to secular personal growth methods in any way. It simply has a different focus and values system. I have been at health-care conferences where secular personal growth proponents have led the group in affirmations and visualizations that were so complex, convoluted, and drawn out that I had great difficulty staying with the exercise and determining what they sought to accomplish. The symbols used by the leaders were very foreign to me as a Christian. The predominant use of crystals, temples, and other cosmic imagery made me uncomfortable, although I recognized that these were likely designed by and for individuals whose belief system included such symbolism. Also, the music was typically so ethereal and synthesized that it became distracting. Music has a place in biblical prayer, of course, but generally simple compositions and accompaniments seem to work best. In both a religious and secular context, it is possible to drown out the message with music or a plethora of words and symbols.

As mentioned in our discussion of *meditatio*, the Christian who is drawn to affirmations, visualizations, or self-esteem enhancement can find plenty of rich food in the

Bible. Not only is the symbolism rich and diverse in the Bible, but it is also profoundly simple. While there is some philosophy in the Bible (e.g. Ecclesiastes), most theorizing is done at a very practical level. The biblical authors are trying to transform rather than impress individuals. They generally used simple concepts and symbols which their audiences would understand.

The symbolism of the Bible is foreign to us mainly because of cultural differences. With a moderate amount of background study, we can decipher biblical symbolism and transpose it into our own historical and cultural understanding. The symbols and morals of the Bible are basically simple; it is living them that is difficult. They are as suitable as any secular resource for building up our self-esteem and personal effectiveness. Further, as the inspired word of God, they possess an authority no secular symbol, moral, or principle can match.

The practice of *lectio divina* inevitably implies a decision and commitment. Like prayer and life, *lectio divina* is to some extent work and discipline. We attempt it even when we don't feel like it, though without carrying it to the point of exhaustion and despair. We will have our good and bad days, just as in anything else.

Faithfulness to *lectio divina* is like attending Church services. Many people stop attending Church because they don't get anything out of it. While I am not advocating pain or total boredom, the focus somehow seems misplaced. We worship privately (e.g. *lectio divina*) or in community because we wish to give something back to God and others. Getting something out of it is secondary. Prayer, *lectio divina*, and indeed all Christian practices are primarily devoted to serving God and others. Personal growth and need fulfillment, however important, are secondary except in matters of personal health. In the mystery of God's plan, our needs and potential are better fulfilled when we put God or others first, without neglecting ourselves.

Through prayer and *lectio divina*, we discover what we truly need, rather than what we simply desire. As Job and Jesus teach us, everything in the Christian's life must be ordered to God's will. Because this inevitably involves the Cross and dying to self, both daily and in extraordinary events, the Christian must at some point take what they can from secular personal growth methods and concepts and enter more deeply into the Christian human potential process. This vocation consists of becoming more like Jesus, and learning the meaning of service, prayer, and perfection in love and obedience through suffering.[18]

SYNOPSIS

Lectio divina disposes us to pray and hear God's word, especially in Scripture and other spiritual literature, but in other daily sacraments as well.[19] It is simple but challenging, equally appropriate for scholar and lay person. No one should be intimidated by it, for it exists solely to bring us closer to God, ourselves, our neighbor, and nature. It is a non-competitive process of becoming more familiar with and faithful to God's word. Its holistic nature consists not only of its integration of mind, body, and spirit, but its balancing of initiative and receptivity.

Job and *lectio divina* are particularly complementary in their conscious and mystical integration of both human (anthropocentric) and divine (theocentric) perspectives and questions. Amid this holistic process of listening, discerning, accepting, and acting upon God's word in Scripture,[20] we can pose inspired questions both to God and ourselves. We can pray and contrast our perspectives, experiences, and responses with the biblical characters, and thereby bring our personal "why's?" under the light of divine inspiration.

Lectio divina empowers us to be active participants in our personal journey of faith. A belief system learned from others but not ingrained in our hearts will not survive the test of dire suffering. The concepts of this or any book on suffering may provide a foundation for reading God's word, but they are no substitute! The sharing of our personal story in light of God's word with both God and others can deepen our relationships, and help us cope with suffering and stress. Our obedient disposition enables God to transform our difficult situation in a redemptive fashion.

Lectio divina should be a challenge for us, rather than a burden. The last thing *lectio divina* wishes to encourage is perfectionism. It disciplines us according to our abilities and resources. Sometimes five minutes with God's word is all we have. Perhaps we have difficulty with the contemplation aspect, and find ourselves stopping with prayer. Whatever our situation, we can ask God to teach us to slow down, listen, and respond. God can work wonders with our crooked paths. The ultimate test of our *lectio divina* is the effect it has on our lives.

An example of *lectio divina* is contained in chapter eleven (*Emmanuel: Where Are We When God Needs Us?*). Although the upcoming reflections on Job are not in *lectio divina* format, they are the by-product of the author's personal and communal experience of *lectio divina* and Job. The reader should not feel constrained to accept any or all of the author's insights. It is hoped that his comments will trigger in the reader their own insights and reflections, including ways in which Joban and biblical concepts can be adapted in practical ways to everyday life experiences.

SUPPLEMENTAL RESOURCES

Readers who wish to pursue *lectio divina* further can consult the following resources: *The Love of Learning and the Desire for God* by Jean LeClerq, O.S.B.[21], *The Benedictine Way* by Wulstan Mork, O.S.B., and *Too Deep for Words: Rediscovering Lectio Divina*, by Thelma Hall, R.C. *Lectio divina* is discussed in most books on monastic spirituality, in particular the Benedictine rule.

Readers may also wish to familiarize themselves with the writings of Cardinal Carlo Maria Martini, S.J., Archbishop of Milan, an internationally respected scriptural scholar and ecumenical leader. Martini utilizes *lectio divina* as the cornerstone of a pastoral religious formation program he calls the "School of the Word." A recent article in which he describes his methodology is included in the appendix. His explanation is the most concise and insightful I have encountered. His works make an excellent companion to this book, and are included in the bibliography.

PASTORAL POSTSCRIPT: WHY LECTIO DIVINA?

Although *lectio divina* has been a Christian devotional practice for centuries, it has rarely been consistently practiced at the parish level, although as discussed earlier Bible readers often progress through its stages without being cognizant of its formal structure. Because both individuals and the community have many demands on their time and energy, it is important that we understand why *lectio divina* is so crucial for today's Christian. The following is a summary of reasons why *lectio divina* is truly a practice for our times.

Practical And Personal

Practicality is the primary reason for including the first two chapters of the book (i.e. *Job, Word of God, and Healing*, and *Lectio Divina*) as a preface to our reflections on Job. While there are many inspirational books that tell individuals' stories of suffering, none of these, however moving, are the inspired word of God. There is an authority and truthfulness behind the word of God that surpasses even the most authentic of human stories. I can hope in the word of God, I can stake my life upon it. I can trust that when Job speaks of life as suffering, there is truth in his statement that needs to be explored. It is more than dogmatic theology or profound philosophy. It is universal truth with personal applications.

As beautiful and healing as human stories and theodicies are in the context of suffering, they do not constitute a personal call like the word of God does. When I am suffering, it is not enough to hear someone else's story of suffering and hope. I want to understand and share my own as well. I want to know where God is in my pain. I want to know why He permitted it, and how He is going to heal me. While I am doubtful of receiving direct answers from God which would remove the need for faith, hope, and trust, I still need to put before God my needs, hopes, and questions, and listen with my mind, body, and spirit for His presence and response. *Lectio divina* facilitates such holistic communication with God, especially when we are suffering. As mentioned in the introduction, the Bible is *the* book of suffering.

Lectio divina is ideal for sufferers because it is simple, flexible, and practical. It can be done in five as well as fifty minutes. Like any commitment, it requires self-discipline. It is a burden only if we make it so. It is complementary, not contradictory, to the rest of our daily activities. For example, how can we manage our time, strengths, weaknesses, and energies if we fail to keep in touch with God's initiative and call in our life? *Lectio divina* provides us with the opportunity to listen to ourselves and become more aware of our overall situation. It slows us down and inspires us to reflect and assess.

Therapeutic And Cathartic

When practiced in a sincere and humble manner, *lectio divina* can be therapeutic and cathartic. While God may be among the first things in the sufferer's mind, religion as law and theology as science are among the last things the sufferer wishes to hear. When people suffer, they don't want to hear pious God-talk that trivializes their situation. Yet, in most persons there is a felt need, either conscious or subconscious, to empty themselves of their deepest feelings about God and their circumstances.

Lectio divina is an excellent framework within which to spill one's guts, for God can take all we can dish out. It is good to go before someone with whom we can be totally honest and secure. Not all human therapists and care-givers can handle the intensity of our thoughts and emotions.

Unlike we human comforters who often imitate Job's friends in dispensing easy answers and recycling pious platitudes, the divine therapist doesn't doubt, psychoanalyze, theologize, criticize, interrupt, or downplay our feelings. He simply listens and offers us healing in His own way and time. Of course, the divine therapist often works through human agents, be they secular or pastoral counselors, individuals we relate to on a daily, occasional, or chance basis, or secular or religious support groups.

Lectio divina is particularly efficacious when there are deep-seated emotions that we are unable to express. As St.

Paul explains in Rm 8:26-27: "Likewise the Spirit helps us in our weakness; for we do not know how to pray as we ought, but that very Spirit intercedes with sighs too deep for words. And God, who searches the heart, knows what is the mind of the Spirit, because the Spirit intercedes for the siants according to the will of God." *Lectio divina* disposes us to receive the Spirit's intercession in our weakness.

Lectio divina can help individuals acknowledge and resolve their anger by revealing in Scripture the wide range of emotions that human beings experience. Rather than repress these emotions, the Christian learns through the Bible to acknowledge and channel them. By seeing that even biblical heroes such as David, Saul, Moses, and Peter can fall, we learn that holiness is no protection against temptation (conversely, it often seems to work as an invitation), and that we are saved by God's mercy, rather than through our own efforts.

Transformational Versus Informational

The objectives of *lectio divina* are transformational in nature. Informational objectives are secondary; they are more relevant to Bible *study*. It is very easy for individual spiritual reading or group Bible sharing to become either a 'head trip' or a theological roller coaster. *Lectio divina* helps us avoid using 'proof texting' to justify either our religious doctrines or our personal disposition and lifestyle. 'Proof texting' places the word of God at our service, rather than vice-versa. When we read the Bible holistically, i.e. with our body (e.g. through proper posture and use of the senses), mind, and spirit, we can avoid 'proof texting' and 'head trip' reading, which are not conducive to balanced spiritual and human growth.

The framework of *lectio divina* (reading/listening, meditation, prayer, and contemplation) constitutes a basic approach to life which we will term in chapter eleven an Emmanuel or God-with-us consciousness. The Christian can meet God in nature, Eucharist, the Sacraments, work, recreation, music, art, etc., and perhaps most profoundly in the suffering person using the above stages as a path for reflecting on the mystery or event at hand. This should not be understood as a mechanical process where the initiative and hard work lies solely with us. God can draw us towards Him in a natural, flowing manner that defies precise description just as easily as He can reward us for our persistence as in the case of Job or the 'persistent widow.'[22] This presumes that we are convinced of God's initiative and presence in the world and in our lives. Finding God in all things is deeply rooted in Christian tradition, and in particular Ignatian and Franciscan paths of spirituality. For an example, refer to St. Ignatius' *Contemplation to Obtain Divine Love* in his Spiritual Exercises.

Lectio Divina *And Christian Spirituality*

It is no secret that Eastern religions and the 'New Age' movement have made considerable inroads into western society as well as the Church. Unbeknownst to many, Christianity has a diverse tradition of spirituality that is anchored in the word of God. We can affirm what is within our own tradition without offending those who choose different belief systems. *Lectio divina* is an excellent foundation for exploring this treasure, for it can bring to life the writings of the saints, Church leaders, and spiritual writers from all eras. It can also lead to greater awareness and appreciation of legitimate forms of culture such as art, music, literature, and nature.

Appropriate for individuals at all levels of faith and responsibility, *lectio divina* is both an evangelical and formational tool that enables individuals and groups to discover how God's word relates to everyday life and their personal and collective experience. *Lectio divina* helps make religion relevant and personal.

Christian Growth And Support Groups

Because the Bible is best understood in community, *lectio divina* is an ideal framework for shared prayer and Scripture reading in a Christian support group environment. Parish programs such as Cardinal Martini's "School of the Word"[23] are an excellent holistic complement to Bible studies concerned with exegesis and learning or prayer groups that emphasize the spirit and emotions. By integrating prayer, Scripture, life experiences, and dialogue, *lectio divina* is a good framework for inspiring commitment on a community level. Both Scripture study and shared prayer have their place within the community, but in our complex world they need to be supplemented with a formational program designed to prepare individuals mind, body, and spirit for the challenges of our times. What better foundation for Christian solidarity, healing, and transformation than God's word?

Christianity And Personal Growth: A 'Back Door' Approach

In the self-help, popular psychology era in which we live, it is understandable that Christians can get swept up in the promises offered by popular writers and motivational speakers, both Christian and secular. Self-help resources understandably make attractive and compelling promises in order to spark interest in their product. Suffering, the cross, and self-abandonment to divine providence are not usually central elements of their philosophies, if only because in our consumption-oriented society these rarely entice and sell.

Christianity is uniquely qualified to offer an alternative perspective on personal growth because of its 'back door' effect. Jesus exhorts us to seek first the kingdom of God and the rest of life's necessities will be added unto us. He departs from mainstream inspirational speakers and writers in offering us true security in heavenly rather than earthly realities. Observance of this leads to a singleness of purpose that distinguishes all great achievers. This presumes that we are willing to work towards emotional and spiritual detachment, and away from an inordinate clinging to material goods and sensory pleasures.

There is such a thing as trying too hard and developing tunnel vision in pursuit of a goal. The Christian approach of partnership with God and faithfulness to a higher cause relieves us of self-imposed burdens, and helps us achieve through the 'back door' what we might have thought impossible. *Lectio divina* can foster personal growth, but this comes as a by-product rather than as a primary objective. The by-products of peace, joy, self-esteem, self-confidence, humor, and self-motivation are legitimate in themselves, but they are not the first fruits. Prayer, Bible reading, works of charity, and communal worship are all primarily oriented towards serving God and others. According to the Beatitudes, we are happiest when we trust in God for the fulfillment of our needs while taking responsible steps to cooperate with His providence.

Our needs and God's will are not mutually exclusive,

although in practice they frequently seem to be. This dichotomy arises from the mystery of human suffering as well as our inability to distinguish needs from desires, and our will and reason from God's plan. The process of coping with these divergences leads to daily and extraordinary crosses. When such crosses arise, we need to cling to the consoling and exhorting word of God for support, guidance, and inspiration.

Job is particularly helpful in this area, for it counteracts the self-centered, falsely optimistic vision of life promoted by many personal growth proponents. The rosy picture of life painted in so many books and workshops makes one wonder whether they are in touch with the grim reality of poverty and other forms of human misery.

The truth about life's unpleasant aspects hurts at first, but accepting the necessity of suffering is the first step towards healing and permitting God to make it redemptive and transformational. It is healthier and more prudent to call manure by its name and convert it to energy, than to expect it to be ice cream and gag while we chew it.

CHAPTER FOUR

The Story Of Job: I Am Job, We Are Job

THE ORIGINS OF JOB: SOCIAL AND RELIGIOUS SETTINGS

The book of Job is one of the world's literary as well as spiritual classics. It has been praised by secular and religious scholars, psychologists, physicians, poets, playwrights, and confirmed atheists. The identity and social background of the author is unknown. Most scholars date Job somewhere between 600 B.C. and 300 B.C. It may have been composed during or soon after the period in which the Jewish people were exiled in Babylon.[24]

Job was born of a suffering people. The long history of suffering for the Hebrew nation can be deduced simply by looking at a map. Palestine, formerly known as the Promised Land or Canaan, is a small but topographically diverse region that has been the haven of conflict since the beginning of civilization. For thousands of years it has been the passage way between Europe, Asia, and Africa. The Hebrews lived at the crossroads of civilization and paid for it. Their history was filled with conflict and bondage. They knew what it meant to suffer.

It is therefore not surprising that the Hebrew Scriptures contain profound insights into human suffering. The Jewish Bible explored and articulated the psycho-spiritual dynamics of suffering long before the advent of modern social sciences. Until Jesus, Job was the Holy Spirit's chief spokesperson on this mystery. The truths revealed by Job are timeless and universal. His words and example speak to the emotions and experiences of each person.

Ancient Literary Counterparts

It is important to note that Job was preceded by the theodicies[25] and literature of other religions and cultures. Babylonian, Sumerian, and Egyptian works on similar themes have been discovered and are frequently compared with Job.[26] The human struggle with the contradictory realities of suffering and a loving God is as old as civilization. Because we are asking the same questions our ancestors did, we would be wise to consider their insights. This especially holds true for the biblical works, since they are held by the Jewish and Christian communities to be the inspired word of God. If you are struggling with God's role in human suffering, why waste time with speculative theories and doctrines? Emulate Job by going to the source: "God, where are you?"

Retribution Doctrine: What Goes Around,
Comes Around

One of the central themes of both Jewish and pagan theodicies was that of retribution. Retribution doctrine specifies that God rewards people according to their deeds. Its pervasive presence in the book of Deuteronomy has given rise to the parallel term "the Deuteronomic principle." Based on this doctrine, suffering came to be regarded as an act of divine retribution, and prosperity as a manifestation of God's approval. Such a life vision would have been intolerable for Jewish persons experiencing excruciating suffering at the hands of ruthless pagans.

Not So, Says Job

The book of Job was born of the spiritual unrest caused by retribution doctrine. It provided a comprehensive yet subtle modification of this philosophy. Retribution doctrine provided black and white answers to explain suffering that were acceptable only if you were not the sufferer. Lest we think we are dealing with an antiquated philosophy, we need only look at the fundamental values which drive modern society. Western society is largely governed by the retribution principle, except that human beings have replaced God as the administrator. The political maneuvering that corrupts business, social, and governmental organizations is ultimately based on the modern principle of retribution: "You scratch my back, I'll scratch yours." While not everyone believes or acts according to this principle, those who dissent enough to make their voices heard are clearly in the minority.

The book of Job responds to retribution with a profound story that challenges its quid pro quo, "what's in it for me" mentality, and proposes a viable alternative. Having set the stage, let us pull up the curtain.

I AM JOB, WE ARE JOB

While Job contains a wealth of theological, psychological, and philosophical wisdom, its main purpose is much more practical and pastoral. Job is an open-ended story designed to serve as a mirror for not only the sufferer and care-giver, but the religious person in general. It is concerned with the believer's attitude towards suffering, justice, religion, and God. The following sketch of the drama illustrates that Job's story is everyone's story, and is especially relevant to the modern sufferer and care-giver.

BLESSED JOB

We begin with a person who is whole, holy, and fabulously wealthy and wise. (Perhaps we know individuals who fit this description, or act like it anyhow?) Naturally, his kids get along great and he gives them space. The communication channels are open, the kids have been trained to do the right thing, and Job has not a trace of possessiveness. He brings his paternal concerns to prayer, rising early in the morning to intercede for his children in case they have unintentionally offended God during their celebrations. These details cause us to wonder: What has this to do with me? I am a broken person whose experience of life has frequently been the opposite of Job's. My career pursuits have come at a high cost. I have been treated unfairly in the business world and in my community. Most of my plans and dreams have gone unfulfilled. My family relationships are fraught with friction and failed expectations. Although my intentions are good, I lack the discipline and energy to rise early and pray for my loved ones.

PORTENTS OF TROUBLE

We are interrupted in our observance of this blessed soul by a royal gathering in heaven and a strange conversation with ominous overtones. Our reaction to God's discussion and subsequent wager with Satan is horror, until we realize that Satan is not the devil of Judeo-Christian tradition, but an angelic adversary responsible for monitoring human activity. We eavesdroppers are divided on the issue raised by the adversary. Some reluctantly accept Satan's view that self-interest underlies all human deeds and motivation. Others affirm Yahweh's confidence that Job, and therefore human beings, are capable of serving God "for nothing," i.e. unconditional love. Some are angry at God's nonchalant acceptance of this seemingly frivolous wager. Those of us with deep wounds caused by inexplicable human tragedies may think to ourselves "That's God for you. He tests and tests you until you feel like you want to die." All are united in disgust at Satan, the perpetrator of this cataclysmic trial.

JOB'S RESILIENCE AMIDST TRAGEDY

In accordance with the heavenly wager, Satan destroys Job's present and future. His fortune is wiped out and his children lie dead amidst the rubble of a natural disaster.

Job's experience is familiar to us, if not in so extreme a manner. Perhaps we have lost children or other close relatives, or have experienced severe business, financial, or career setbacks. On the outside we seem to have coped, but inwardly we nurture angry feelings towards God, life, and perhaps others. Job's willingness to bless the Lord when He takes away astounds us. We know how we resent the stripping away of things precious to us, especially when it seems contrary to God's will (e.g. a freak accident or deliberate human violence). If God is all-powerful, why would He permit this? Where is God when you need Him? How can we speak of God as provident when we suffer this tragedy and deprivation? If this is His will, He can keep it!

DOUBLE "FOR NOTHING"

We return to heaven where a repeat of the previous celestial scene occurs, this time with God agreeing to Job's physical destruction. We are puzzled at God's boastful demeanor and His continued participation in such pointless games being played with human lives. Perhaps God's acceptance of the second wager unearths repressed images of a capricious God that we learned as a child or through negative experiences with religious persons or institutions. If we have or are experiencing intense physical, psychological, or spiritual pain, we recoil at the thought of anyone, especially God, reacting so nonchalantly to suffering.[27]

KING OF THE HILL

Isolated from the community and in excruciating physical pain, Job reigns on the dung heap. Mrs. Job (an often overlooked victim of Satan's cynicism and God's compliance) speaks for angry sufferers everywhere when she tells Job to let go of his integrity and curse God. From her perspective, God is undeserving of human faithfulness and respect. Job rebukes her and rhetorically asks if we should not take the good with the bad. Their subsequent words and feelings are left to our imagination.

We might agree with Job in theory but not in practice. There is something in the human spirit that rebels against such total devastation of human life. Job is an ideal but unreal model of faith.

MODEL COMFORTERS

Job's friends arrive and perform the mourning rituals in a sincere and compassionate manner. They are overwhelmed at the sight of Job, whom they initially do not recognize. They express their solidarity with Job through tears and physical gestures of empathy. They are present to him in silence for the prescribed mourning period of seven days. They reveal themselves to be faithful friends who are willing to share in his pain. They unashamedly become Job's court on the ignominious dung heap.

THE GREAT LAMENT

This heart-rending union of silent, confused mourners is starkly interrupted by Job's cry of anguish and desperation. When we hear him express his total desolation and hatred of life, a part of ourselves seconds his lament. As our imagination absorbs the profound images of despair uttered by Job, we begin to experience bitterness over the painful realities of life. We recall the tragedies and disappointments we have experienced. With Job we ask: Why should life be like this? If such is the case, is life worth living?

THEOLOGICAL BOXING: THREE ROUNDS OR TILL EXHAUSTION

Eliphaz, Job's eldest and wisest friend, politely requests permission to speak. He answers Job's lament with a moral and religious exhortation that is good in intent and theory, but atrocious in execution and timing. We are stunned at his pomposity until we recognize that we are likewise tempted to offer easy answers to persons in pain.

Eliphaz is later joined by his friends Bildad and Zophar. Together they unwittingly recycle dry, black and white, theological and moral panaceas. Their transformation from model comforters to self-appointed divine spokesmen seems to be triggered by Job's uncomplimentary reference to God and orthodox doctrine. The increasing intensity of their tone and content suggests that Job's unorthodox language threatened their religious perspective. The friends become a classic example of human decency and compassion being subordinated to dogma and orthodoxy. They vehemently defend God at the expense of the suffering Job. The friends' mentality is evident anywhere comforters profess to have the answer or path necessary for the sufferer's cure without having experienced the affliction themselves. Their poor timing, insensitivity, and misguided zeal overshadow their sincere intentions.

During their dialogue Job spoke *to* God, while the friends spoke *about* and *for* Him. Job drew his responses from experience and the heart, the friends from dogmas and the head. The friends' primary mistake was their refusal to take risks out of compassion for Job. There is security in affirming commonly held religious or moral propositions. Thank God for people like Job who thirst for the truth about God and life even when it takes them on unblazed paths!

In fairness to the friends, listening patiently to Job might in their minds have implied approval of his wild, unorthodox sayings. Were they to empathize with Job, they might have felt themselves to be risking the wrath of God, who would undoubtedly be intolerant of such arrogant and antagonizing language. Prudence dictated that they save both their own and Job's skin by discouraging such talk and thereby not rocking the theological boat.

JOB'S EXPANDED CONSCIOUSNESS

As Job develops his complaint, affirming his innocence and taking God to task for His capriciousness and cruelty, he begins to focus on the universality of innocent suffering. It had surrounded him in the past, and he had expressed his sympathy in laudable, practical fashion. Yet, while performing heroic acts of kindness for the downtrodden, he had never taken issue with God over their plight. In his blessed state it was difficult for him to relate to their situation. Their emotions and life perspective were foreign to him.

Job's religious formation was rooted in the theology of the Hebrew Wisdom movement. Chief among the tenets of Wisdom theology was retribution doctrine, which stated that good actions beget good results, and bad actions beget bad results. If this seemed not to be the case, the innocent sufferer is encouraged to "wait on the Lord."[28] God would eventually administer justice. Innocent suffering was a temporary situation which would be corrected by God.

Retribution doctrine affirmed the status quo and thus served the needs of those in comfortable positions.

Job's plight takes him deeper into the world of innocent suffering, this time as a participant. He begins to recognize the limitations and exceptions to retribution doctrine present in the mass injustices that permeate human existence. In taking the focus off himself and finding other subjects worthy of attention, Job enters deeper into the mysteries of life and suffering. In his journey towards compassion, he looks to God for some insight into the meaning of his suffering.

THE WISDOM POEM

In the midst of their raging debate, our combatants are interrupted by a poetic insertion that effectively renders their arguments void. According to this intrusive voice, human beings lack the wisdom necessary to comprehend the great mysteries of life. Only those who revere God and avoid evil are on the path towards Wisdom, which is personified as a companion to God at the time of creation. Interestingly, the words used in 28:28 to describe wise human behavior were repeatedly applied to Job in the prologue. Perhaps the poem is subtly suggesting that Job is on the path to Wisdom, though he may not know it.

For many readers, the Wisdom Poem is a misplaced and deficient anticlimax. We are left without any practical clue as to how the believer is to comprehend and respond to innocent suffering. Initially we view the Wisdom Poem as a truthful non-answer satisfying neither Job nor the reader. With hindsight, however, we can see how it prepares us for the transcendent wisdom of an unexpected visitor soon to make the scene.

JOB'S CLOSING ARGUMENT

With the debate apparently rendered pointless, Job's next speech carries a more personal and passionate tone. Turning his attention from the friends, he engages in a public examination of conscience. We are invited to empathize with Job as he reviews his dramatic fall from grace despite his impeccable integrity. He has done all the right things while experiencing the most horrifying of results.

Perhaps we see ourselves emulating Job in presenting God with a litany of good deeds and dashed hopes. We join Job in stating our case in the hope that an impartial arbiter (perhaps God himself) will step between us and God and administer justice.[29] Job's passion for his integrity and honor is undeterred by the prospect of facing God. After laying everything on the line, he concludes his testimony by signing his complaint. There is nothing left to say.

A DAWN MATCH AND A CHALLENGE FROM THE CROWD

With Job and his friends exhausted, the young upstart Elihu joins in and proceeds to rebuke both parties for their inadequate theology. Though his theology is slightly more refined than the friends', he comes no closer to penetrating the mystery of suffering. His zealousness and inexperience betray him, and he is unable to provide any breakthrough insight on Job's sad state of affairs. This is not surprising in light of the Wisdom Poem's testimony. Nothing short of a theophany[30] would seem to resolve the case.

AN UNEXPECTED VISITOR STORMS IN

To Job's and his friends' astonishment, a thundering voice arises from a whirlwind and addresses Job. Would Job's hopes for a direct vindication be fulfilled? Fortunately for Job and ourselves, No! In lieu of a simple resolution, God reveals the incomprehensible to Job through a series of challenges, questions, and profound images. Rather than give Job a reason or justification for his suffering, He diverts Job's attention to the big picture of life. God asks Job to go beyond himself and his problems for the purpose of observing God's inscrutable administration of the world. While assuring Job that the world is not returning to chaos, God repels Job's criticism of His justice and cosmic plan by reversing the scenario and becoming the questioner rather than the questioned. Rather than reveal divine wisdom or secrets, Yahweh invites Job to contemplate the glory of God, and Job's relationship to Creator and creation. Instead of removing the need for faith, Yahweh brings it to the fore. The Wisdom Poem had anticipated this revelation by testifying that only God can comprehend the profound mysteries that Job and his friends were discussing. God's answer to Job is a personal call to recognize His involvement in the world even in the midst of suffering. The central reality in life is God. He is the prism through which everything must be seen, even suffering.

It is easy to appreciate the theology underlying God's response when we are not in the midst of suffering. When it becomes our turn to suffer, both rational and pious interpretations may ring hollow in our ears. If the rational and the theological are insufficient, where can we turn?

JOB'S RESPONSE

To our great surprise, Job is not only satisfied but transformed by Yahweh's challenging response. God has neither addressed Job's grievances nor affirmed his innocence. He has simply diverted Job's attention from his pain, and honored his request for a personal encounter. In response, Job retracts his lawsuit while disavowing his harsh lament about the human condition.[31] God's assurance of His sovereignty is so convincing that Job offers a personal statement of faith extolling God's wisdom, providence, and power, along with Job's relative ignorance.

ASSESSING THE TURNABOUT

Job had previously anticipated the modern existential philosophers in asserting the meaninglessness and intolerable injustices of life. He had doubted God's integrity, but never his own. Now he reverses that judgment. The reader is left to wonder: What got into Job? What did Job hear or experience that caused such an about-face? This was a person who had come within a gnat's eyelash of cursing God.

It is not enough to theorize about Job's transformation. These theories will be empty when I am the sufferer. Somehow I have to get beyond the rational explanations and experience God's response as if it were addressed to me. The next chapter will suggest some avenues through which this is possible.

CHAPTER FIVE

The Morals Of The Story

The climax of Job is universally recognized to be its final five chapters: The Yahweh Speeches, Job's acceptance speech, and the epilogue. As we will see, the epilogue resolves the various subplots developed during the story. In order to synthesize the ending with the events that have gone before, we will follow the example of Job and approach the mystery through a series of questions.

FIRST, what are the primary themes and implications of Yahweh's response? What is its message for both Job and the twentieth century sufferer?

SECOND, why is Job transformed by God's seemingly evasive and abrasive speech? Is there anything in his experience of God and revitalized faith and attitude that can inspire or instruct us?

THIRD, what is the significance of Yahweh's description of Job as His servant who has spoken rightly of Him? What message can we derive from God's dissatisfaction with the friends, who spend all their time and energy defending God and religious orthodoxy?

FOURTH, does the Epilogue depart from the realistic tone of the book when it depicts Yahweh restoring Job twofold?

FINALLY, what is the predominant theme or central message of the book?

Our answers to these questions will determine the place this book occupies in our hearts and daily lives.

FROM RETRIBUTION TO RECONCILIATION

Being not only a literary and theological genius but a pragmatist, the author of Job issues a subtle but simple challenge through his resolution of the story: Live by the call to reconciliation rather than the law of retribution. We have seen that the story began with a conflict between God and Satan over the possibility of unconditional human love and service. The author of Job sides with God in believing that it is possible, though he is aware of the contrary evidence and obstacles to such love. His job will be to convince his audience.

The most practical form of unconditional love is reconciliation, loving when it hurts, when we have to let go of our pride and propensity for self-preservation. This constitutes taking another back into our hearts, perhaps even God, when we can find no rational or emotional justification for this action.

The act of reconciliation is in direct contradiction to that of retribution, which in some respects is a euphemism for retaliation. Human beings are tempted to use retribution doctrine as a theological justification for getting even with those who offend us, or those whom we envy because of what we consider their undeserved prosperity. Like Job, we feel our goodness entitles us to a claim on God and His proper execution of justice. Our integrity becomes a bargaining chip for what we think we deserve. Because such thinking is so natural to human beings, the author uses subtle expressions and colorful images to reveal a different path to human wholeness and holiness. Beginning with the Yahweh Speeches, we will explore the path navigated by the author.

THE INADEQUACY OF RETRIBUTION DOCTRINE

While there are an abundance of themes one could explore in the Yahweh Speeches, perhaps the lesson most relevant to ancient and modern humanity is that concerning the limitations of human wisdom and retribution doctrine. Let us briefly review what has occurred until now as the context within which the Yahweh Speeches occur.

In accordance with retribution doctrine, Job has concluded that his suffering must be the result of sin, yet he is unaware of any such transgressions, especially in proportion to the pain he has suffered. His conclusion is that God's justice has failed. The friends' perspective is similar except they presume Job's guilt.

In exposing the grave misjudgments made by the zealous friends, the author issues a subtle warning to religious people of his own as well as our time: Be slow to judge. Every case is different. Be prudent and compassionate when you apply religious or moral doctrines to pastoral situations. Were religious persons to absorb this message, the whole complexion of institutional religion and pastoral life would be changed, with ripple effects in society as well. Rather than expect other people to change, we should try to refrain from judgment and first examine our own weaknesses. Yet, this is much easier to state in theory than to implement in practice, especially when you are the one offended or threatened.

A SILENT VINDICATION

God's refusal to comment on Job's culpability is an implicit rejection of retribution as an explanation for Job's trials. It can even be seen as an implicit affirmation of Job's integrity in light of God's previous[32] and subsequent[33] extolling of Job before his angelic and human accusers. If I accuse someone of something, and they find the accusation absurd, they may answer with the following: "I won't dignify that comment with a response." From God's perspective, the question of Job's integrity is moot in light of the more crucial issues at hand. God's unwillingness to play the blame game suggests that we would be misguided to waste our energy pointing fingers in response to accidents, mistakes, or tragedies.

As the Wisdom Poem so eloquently stated, human wisdom is ultimately bankrupt when it comes to life's great questions. The big picture of human suffering is so much greater than we can comprehend. Events are so interrelated and scenarios so complex that rational analysis of any situation beyond a certain point (where you've learned all you can from the incident) is speculation that leads to frustration.

APPLYING JOB'S EXONERATION TO OUR SCRUPLES

The challenging tone of Yahweh's response indicates that if He had a correction to make, He would not be shy about it. We can apply this insight as follows: When God is silent in our lives, and like Job we are unaware of any particular sin or vice that we are shamelessly committing, we can confidently let go of all inclination to ruthlessly cross-examine ourselves. In such situations honesty is the best policy. We can tell God we are unaware of any major transgressions, but that if we have a particular blind spot, would He please reveal this to us? If there is something He desires to bring to our attention, we await His word. God's subsequent affirmation of Job's blunt honesty and His disapproval of the friends' flowery God-talk[34] indicates that He much prefers straight shooters to pompous theologians in the matter of prayer. If we are worried, angry, or depressed about something, we should tell Him. Likewise if we are relieved, happy, or excited. We should talk to God even if we don't feel we get anything out of it. Consider the wisdom of Rabbi Abraham Heschel: "There is something far greater than my desire to pray — that is, God's desire that I pray."

GRADUAL TRANSFORMATION

It is important to recognize the elements of time and communication in the healing process undergone by Job. Job's response to Yahweh's first speech is one of awe rather than intimacy, a human being overwhelmed by his God.[35] God is apparently not satisfied with Job's humble silence, for it may represent more of a resignation or fearful acquiescence to the divine will than a heartfelt acceptance. God desires a response born of faith and love rather than intimidation. He wants us to be humble out of wonder and trust rather than fear. God knows that there are various motives for obedience, not all of them healthy or holy. As we become more intimate with God through life and prayer, our fear of Him is gradually transformed into love and trust.

In response to Job's fearfulness, it may be helpful to look at our experience of religious formation. Most likely we have been both victim and perpetrator of religious values, actions, and beliefs grounded in fear. We do not start out with perfect love. We do not begin human relationships at the level of intimacy, so why should we expect this with God? Perhaps we bear scars from religious persons whose actions towards us were ultimately motivated by self-interest or self-preservation. Underlying their motives may be a profound fear, distrust, and subtle resentment of God. Job's friends fit this category. If we look deeply enough into our hearts, we may find traces of this in ourselves as well.

Because we usually do not encounter God in so dramatic a manner, we might ask ourselves how Job's experience is relevant to our personal situation and manner of praying. The answer is one that has been discovered by religious persons since the beginning of time: Contemplation. Contemplation is the receptive, God-centered, listening aspect of prayer. Before we consider the nature of this contemplation, let us pause briefly to remind ourselves of a prerequisite of both contemplation and Job's gradual transformation: Patience.

OUR TIMING AND PLANS ARE NOT NECESSARILY GOD'S

Despite Job's wholeness and holiness, it took time for God to get His message across. If God needs time and suffering to mold Job, will He not require the same for us? Perhaps we can remember this when along our journey we discover that our faith is not what we thought, and that God has much pruning to do. How much more gentle and patient we ought to be both with ourselves and others!

LISTENING AND PRAYER

God perfects Job's faith through both active and receptive elements of communication. Both Job and God need to speak their piece. As in all human communications, it is essential that both parties listen. The Scriptures frequently speak of the dynamics of listening on both God's part and ours. Let us briefly examine the general principles Scripture puts before us.

Regarding God's listening, the overwhelming testimony of Scripture is that God hears our prayer. This was a central element of Jesus' teaching. He proposed numerous parables illustrating God's receptivity to human prayer.[36] In tension with this is the human experience of seemingly unanswered prayers. This experience of rejection and abandonment is referred to in various parts of the Hebrew Scriptures, most notably the Psalms. When God's response or lack thereof thoroughly confounds us, we conclude that He has not heard our prayer. If God had heard our prayer, surely things would have turned out differently. At other times we recognize that He has responded to our prayer, but we don't like His answer.

As is often the case in Scripture, there is a voice in tension with the experience of abandonment described above. It speaks of God's transcendent wisdom and word, and the inability of human beings to comprehend the divine plan. Examples of this are the Wisdom Poem in Job (chapter

28) and various passages in Isaiah, a work paralleling Job in both literary beauty and prophetic vision.

To retain a balanced perception of the dynamics of God's disposition towards human prayer, the various voices in Scripture must be kept in healthy tension. The tension between our human experience of abandonment and the call to trust in God's fidelity is at the core of biblical faith. It constitutes a lifelong challenge for the believer. Job's suffering thrusts him into this paradox. He exemplifies the two sides of the human experience of God's response to prayer. At certain points he is confident God will hear him. At other times he seems to have lost hope in God's willingness to listen and rectify his situation.

In conclusion, the Scriptures have a two-pronged message concerning God's disposition towards our prayer. First, He always listens, and responds in a way that is best for us. Second, this is not always evident in our circumstances, thereby causing us considerable consternation. The moral seems to be that we persist in asking, questioning, and sharing our thoughts and emotions with God. In His time, He will act.[37]

Do We Listen Selectively Or Obediently?

Fundamentally related to God's speaking is our hearing. We know that our hearing is inconsistent. We are often selectively open to God's agenda. Sometimes only the discipline of suffering and God's compassion can enlarge our hearts to learn and obey His word. Whether God says "Yes," "No," "Not yet," or "You decide," we can resolve to persist in listening for His activity and presence in our lives. This openness to God, manifested in an interior silence before Him, is called contemplation.

SUFFERING AS OPPORTUNITY FOR CONTEMPLATION

Contemplation is an invitation to simplicity and other-centeredness. It is the spiritual alternative to both religious and secular easy answers. Throughout his speeches, Job had contemplated various aspects of human existence from the sufferer's perspective. The fruit of this contemplation was Job's increased awareness of innocent suffering. Contemplation led Job out of his misery into consideration of the solidarity he shared with others who suffer innocently. Oddly enough, his religious friends were blinded by their dogmas from joining him in this vision.

While we naturally look at suffering from an anthropocentric (humanity-centered) or egocentric (I-centered) perspective, God reveals to Job and to us that this view is limited, and can lead to distortion. Human emotions and personal experiences are a natural and healthy point of departure for our journey to God, but they are ultimately insufficient for human fulfillment. God invites Job to contemplate life from His perspective. The Wisdom Poem anticipated this insight. The Yahweh Speeches place before us food for contemplation designed to draw us out of our limited perspective.

CONTEMPLATION AND PERSONAL GROWTH

If we can be brought out of ourselves, our eyes will be opened to both the wonder and contradictions that surround us. We can acknowledge that life is full of mysteries, both joyous and tragic, which are beyond human comprehension. If we look at life purely from a human standpoint, we could easily be overwhelmed by pleasure or sorrow, depending on our circumstances at the time. God's perspective provides a balanced context for experiencing life. If true wisdom lies solely with God, as the Wisdom Poem asserts, we need to grow in intimacy with God in order to approach life in a wise manner. The Scriptures, the Christian community, prayer, and life experiences are powerful resources for developing this intimacy with God.

Perhaps the major weakness of the modern personal growth movement is its inability to come to terms with the contradictions of human existence. Human potential literature frequently focuses on what we can do without encouraging a deep consciousness of what is beyond our reach. Such a self-sufficient attitude is at odds with the biblical perspective, especially as revealed in Job.

The Christian approach to human development integrates the anthropocentric and theocentric perspectives, and is centered in the incarnation and paschal mystery. Everything of consequence is measured in the light of the incarnation, suffering, death, and resurrection of Jesus Christ.

The natural superiority of the Christian approach is demonstrated most powerfully in response to suffering. For Christians, the pain of suffering is an unpleasant consequence of human disobedience and natural forces, but through Christ it has become the seed of salvation. This redemptive aspect of suffering distinguishes the Christian from the secular approach, and its efficacy has been demonstrated in the lives of countless living and dead saints.

The personal growth movement can be directed towards gratification of either legitimate or distorted human needs and desires. Christians must therefore be discerning in their absorption and application of secular personal growth concepts, methods, and values. The fundamental issue is whether the approach in question is compatible with Christian teaching and values. Generally, if it leaves room for the centrality of the cross and resurrection, and does not contradict fundamental Christian beliefs and values, it is acceptable. An excellent comparison of the Christian and secular perspectives on human development is Cardinal Leon-Joseph Suenen's work *Nature and Grace*, published by Servant Books.

The Scriptures, Tradition, and the Christian community testify to God, not humanity, as the ultimate source and catalyst of human development. If we wish to fulfill our personal calling or vocation, and therefore our potential, we should both start and end with God, complemented by human wisdom, responsible actions, and communal efforts.

A CALL TO I-THOU RELATIONSHIPS[38]

In God's first speech,[39] He illustrates His providence and administration of nature. In His second speech,[40] He articulates His relationship to Job, the wicked, and the forces of chaos. By implication, Job's relationship to these entities is also revealed. Job, like us, needs to know where both we and God stand in relationship to these entities. Each of these relationships merits our attention. From the Judeo-Christian perspective, life and human vocation consists primarily of relationships. The quality of these relationships will determine the quality of our lives and service. All suffering occurs as a result of some distortion or abuse of these relationships. Let us briefly examine each of these relationships from a contemplative standpoint, drawing on insights both from common human experience and the book of Job.

RELATIONSHIPS WITH OTHER PERSONS

We will never properly understand our relationship with others unless we include God as an essential element. Through the gift of contemplation, we can struggle to maintain a spirit of moderation and gratitude in these relationships. We can experience joy and wonder through other persons by continually reminding ourselves of the profound and priceless gifts God has given us in the person of our neighbors and loved ones. It is both sobering and motivational to realize that God does not give us these gifts forever. They are meant to be cherished and appreciated while we have them.

We take far too much for granted in this area. We are often not satisfied with the mere presence of other people. We are losing the ability to use our senses to experience and appreciate their unique beauty. Too often we wait until people depart to reflect on the meaning they gave to our lives. Why wait to say, "Thanks!", "Wow!", and "I love you!"? Don't put off experiencing the simple joys of the presence and personalities of others. Don the eyes of God and see the good in other people without masking the bad. Let go of the Satan-inspired disposition to maintain a defensive, critical tone in interactions with others.

Don't focus solely on the negative aspects of persons and relationships. Give them a dose of the positive! See the beauty of God in everyone you meet, including yourself, not by looking for big things, but by becoming aware of simple, humble beauty marks: a smile, the twinkle of an eye, a considerate gesture, a gentle manner, a witty sense of humor. By asking God for the gift of the Holy Spirit, who can help us perceive and respond to other persons in a healthy and holy manner, we can gradually lift our relationships to an inspired plane. This will not, of course, spare us from the misunderstandings, frustrations, and other problems inherent in human relationships. Rather, it will help us accept, work through, and transcend these realities, and see them in a more positive, hopeful light.

GOD: ADVOCATE OR ADVERSARY?

Job 40:8 presents a profound, and humbling, existential question that is worthy in itself of contemplation. God's question to Job, and by implication all sufferers, is simply, "Would you put me in the wrong so as to justify yourself? Do you need to proclaim your integrity at my expense?"

Too often we assume that what is most important to us is automatically contrary to the plan of God. We view Him as a celestial party-pooper. Like Job, we see Him as our adversary, and proceed to hurl accusations at Him. God is asking Job and us to look at the absurdity of these accusations. He asks us to recognize that our dignity and integrity, however priceless, do not entitle us to challenge His integrity or make demands on Him. This is quite humbling.

God is not automatically disposed or opposed to our plans and dreams. Everything depends on the situation and God's wisdom. We need to integrate enthusiasm with discernment rather than apathy with skepticism. Part of the problem is that God's timetable, objectives, and methods are not always ours. Consequently, we get anxious and impatient.

God is placing before Job and ourselves a choice between pride and friendship. We can either hold on to our anger and close ourselves off from God, or express it and let it go. We can assert ourselves at His expense or humbly submit to our circumstances and the care of divine providence.

Submission to God in self-abandonment does not imply that we become passive or irresponsible in seeking justice. It simply means that we respect the limits to which we are subjected in pursuing justice. Once we do all we can to secure justice, whether for ourselves or others, we must turn things over to God. There is a point where we need to become silent in self-abandonment before Him, replacing our anger and pleas for deliverance with petitions for the gift of trust and acceptance.

It was Job, not Yahweh, who defined their relationship to be adversarial. Job, not Yahweh, pronounced their respective integrities mutually exclusive. How much better on ourselves, God, and those around us when we relate to God as a friend amid our suffering!

CONTEMPLATING NATURE AND THE BEASTS OF CHAOS

Yahweh would undoubtedly affirm the perspective of St. Francis of Assisi and St. Ignatius of Loyola who discovered God in all things. Perhaps He would feel bad for those who reject the element of mystery and ascribe the workings of the universe solely to the laws of nature. How much we miss when we overlook nature's potential to inspire contemplation! How fruitless our fears of chaotic beasts[41] that are part of God's creation just as we are![42] How much more respect and appreciation we would have for all living creatures if we were to adopt a more incarnational perspective in which we looked for God in everything!

LEAVING THE WICKED TO GOD

In 40:9-14 Yahweh briefly comments on Job's outrage at the good fortune of the wicked. His challenge assumes the form of questions which may be summarized as follows: "Can you do a better job than I? Do you have the ability to humble the wicked as I do?"

During his dialogue with the friends, Job had acknowledged God's power over the wicked, but had questioned His seemingly inconsistent use of it. God's answer exposes Job's impotence in this area: He will take Job's criticisms seriously when Job is wise and powerful enough to administer justice.

In trying to mandate divine justice, Job is usurping the privilege of God. Since Job can't execute his judgments, he is better off leaving the matter to God. Interpreters have frequently noted that there appears to be an element of play in God's response. In contrast to Job and his dour friends, could Yahweh have a sense of humor? Perhaps He found some of Job's outrageous claims funny instead of offensive. He knew they arose from truthfulness, integrity, and human weakness rather than self-seeking and malicious intent. Job was simply acting upon the expectations implicit in retribution doctrine.

Human beings are demonstrably incompetent in judging themselves and executing justice, yet they want to manage God's domain. It would be hilarious if it weren't so tragic.

God's response has implications for those who would prescribe strict boundaries and rules for Him. God does execute judgment on the wicked, but not according to human standards and schedules. We lack the wisdom, power, and goodness necessary to render and implement such important judgments. While this truth is palatable in theory, accepting it in the real world can be another story, especially if you or a loved one are victimized by human cruelty and violence.

God's defense of His power is somewhat thinner in logic, length, and imagery than the justifications and illustrations of His wisdom and providence. In my opinion this is because God prefers to conquer and convince through love and free human assent rather than force. Actions speak louder than words. The crucifixion of Jesus completes this passage by revealing God's kingdom commencing through the power of love.

CONTEMPLATION AS THE FOUNDATION OF HEALTHY RELATIONSHIPS

We have seen that God's message to Job is relationship oriented. He started out with nature and progressed to the wicked and the creatures of chaos, with Job's attitude toward God and these entities as an undercurrent.

When asked what are the essential elements of healthy and enduring relationships, or of coping with suffering, our first thought is usually not contemplation. Yet, we have shown how contemplation must be an integral element of our relationships, lest they be distorted by our passions, failings, and ulterior motives. The following is one application of contemplation in action.

CONTEMPLATING BEAUTY: EXERCISE

An essential element of contemplation in daily life is sensitivity. Sensitivity connotes an awareness of life and its various components through the five senses. Our faculties of taste, smell, touch, hearing, and vision enable us to experience life through the physical as well as the mental and spiritual dimensions. It is tragic that in our sensual age so much of the potency of the senses has been lost through over-stimulation, exploitation, and, especially in the western cultures, too much 'living in the head.' From childhood we develop standards of beauty that are more influenced by cultural programming than by our native senses. We need to make a conscious effort to counter this stifling and manipulative programming.

To bring Job's experience of contemplation into our personal universe, we might try the following. Look at a person, element of nature, or material object, and use your senses to become aware of its various qualities. Experience, rather than criticize or interpret, the subject. Render no judgment on the subject other than to appreciate its many aspects. Try to use each of the five senses in your contemplation. Let yourself enjoy or admire the object as it is. Perhaps you will discover things you never noticed before.

If you prefer to stick more closely to the text, try the following. Select a particular image, verse, or passage from the Yahweh Speeches and engage in contemplation of it with your mind, body, and spirit. For example, you might choose Yahweh's description of the war horse in 39:19-25 or the sea in 38:8-11. Begin your contemplation with a period of silence. Precede or follow this with a short prayer asking for the gifts of contemplation, discernment, and acceptance. Ask God to help you let go of both past and future and be present to the moment. Read the text slowly aloud, repeating it several times to ingrain it in your being. Open yourself to a greater appreciation of the subject(s) described in the text using your senses, imagination, and intuition.

This exercise is designed solely to permit the biblical image or message to penetrate your consciousness in a transformational way through the path of prayer and contemplation. Don't choke yourself with expectations. Simply let the text speak to you in a natural fashion. In matters of prayer and contemplation, method is always secondary to sincerity of intent and effort.

AN ALTERNATIVE PERSPECTIVE ON THE YAHWEH SPEECHES

Before we proceed to Job's acceptance speech, it is only fair to ask how we might regard these speeches if we did not see them as invitations to contemplation and transformation of consciousness. As with all aspects of Job, there are a myriad of interpretations and perspectives on the Yahweh Speeches. Many interpreters view the Yahweh Speeches from a much less contemplative perspective. Some are dismayed by God's aggressive response and His refusal to exonerate Job explicitly. Taken literally, the God of the Yahweh Speeches is characterized more by transcendence than tenderness. We have taken a contemplative approach to the text; a more literal interpretation of the speeches is also legitimate and raises important questions.

If we take these speeches at face value and view them as a stern rebuke, we are left with a serious problem in our relationship with God. Does He want blind faith independent of intimacy, where we obey only because He's God and we're not? Where does gentleness and trust come into play? Are we to be fearful servants of God, simple yes-persons who go through life in unquestioning obedience? If God wishes to intimidate rather than persuade us, what is left of our freedom and integrity? Are we to be persuaded through ordinance of authority or invitation to contemplation? Perhaps Job's acceptance speech will shed some light on the matter.

JOB'S ACCEPTANCE SPEECH

Job's acceptance speech[43] is an excellent example of the role of personal encounter in the process of religious transformation. It is significant that it is given in very simple, faith-filled terms that touch on the fundamental tenets of Jewish and Christian faith. The themes articulated by Job are God's wisdom, providence, power, and Job's relative ignorance. The absoluteness and profundity of Job's response inspires us to ask: What moved Job to transcend the miserable state of his reality and praise God in so convincing a manner? What triggered his change of mind?

Self-Abandonment To Divine Providence

The underlying attitude of Job's acceptance speech is self-abandonment to God's will (or divine providence, to use the expression of Father J.P. de Caussade, whose spiritual classic, *Self-Abandonment to Divine Providence*, is highly recommended to readers of Job). The common Christian expression of turning one's life over to Christ is a modern equivalent. Self-abandonment stands in direct contrast to self-sufficiency. It asserts that of ourselves we have neither the answers nor the capability for human fulfillment. We therefore entrust ourselves totally to God's care. Self-abandonment represents the summit of human potential, for it constitutes our active recognition that we can fulfill our vocation only in cooperation with the Lord. St. Ignatius' prayer in the *Contemplation to Obtain Divine Love* is also Job's: "Take, Lord, and receive all my liberty, my memory, my understanding and my entire will. All that I am and possess you have given me. I return it all to you, Lord. All is yours, to be disposed of according to your will. Give me your love and grace, and this suffices."

Job's Contemplative Response

Job's acceptance speech[44] is a profound summary of biblical faith in light of suffering. Because it is composed in such succinct, personal terms (note the predominance of the first person), each verse of Job's statement is excellent material for contemplation.

Because time is not an explicit element in the book of Job, we do not know whether his response was immediate or gradual. Since Job is not a story of instant transformation, it is doubtful that the author intended to communicate a smooth conversion. Instead he poses a plethora of reflection-provoking questions without providing straightforward answers, thus giving his audience the opportunity to sort them out for themselves. Job's response challenges us to reflect upon these questions:

1. Do I agree in both mind and heart with each of Job's assertions? What are my gut-level feelings about each article of faith professed by Job? If I disagree, what prompts me to respond in this way? What emotions, beliefs, or experiences underlay my reaction? Am I willing to share my response with God, then perhaps with a trusted confidant?

2. Why did Yahweh's response inspire Job to such an overwhelming and gratuitous testimony of faith? Would they

have moved me to a similar confession? How would my
reaction have been different?

3. What aspects of the Yahweh Speeches touch me person-
    ally? Do they inspire me to contemplation?[45]

    There is no reason why we can't restate Job's acceptance
    speech in our own words and images, as if the Yahweh
    Speeches were addressed to us. Taking a cue from Job, we
    should respond as honestly as we can. If we feel less
    convinced than Job, recall that few of us possess the
    integrity that Job did. After all, his virtue is deliberately
    exaggerated to support the author's thesis that retribu-
    tion doctrine does not fully explain suffering.

    The mysteries of life, suffering, and divine justice must
ultimately be left to faith, prayer, and contemplation. In the
epilogue, the author will teach us a way to live with these
mysteries.

CHAPTER SIX

Job's Happy Ending

The beauty and wholeness of Job's heart-felt confession of faith in 42:1-6 seemingly leaves us with a fitting completion to the story. Job still suffers, but his personal encounter with God enables him to hold on to his faith and integrity. Job can now peacefully co-exist with God, who is no longer perceived as his adversary.

Let us briefly review what has already occurred. Despite enduring unbearable suffering at the hands of both earthly and heavenly adversaries, Job continues to seek an audience with God. When the encounter is granted, God echoes Elihu's attempts to lead Job out of self-absorption and into awe and wonder at the totality of God's magnificence. Job is admonished by God not for his moral guilt but for his questioning of God's wisdom, providence, and justice.[46]

Job had posed questions to God while neglecting the questions God was posing to him through the circumstances of his life. In this he was corrected, but not condemned. He was challenged, but not degraded. Job's questions had been put into a universal and theocentric context. God is more magnificent than Job had conceived. Overwhelmed and

reassured by God's word and presence, Job gives his acceptance speech, and all seems well. Job has found God and
peace. The story seemingly could end here.

THE BEST SURPRISE IS LAST

As we relax and catch our breath after these startling
revelations, we are alerted that a subplot to Job's suffering
has arisen. Our attention returns to the friends, whose
dogmatic theology and easy answers we have endured for
umpteen chapters. Apparently a serious grievance has
arisen between God and the friends. Eliphaz and his two
friends (Elihu is ignored) are twice rebuked for "not speaking what is right," and Job is twice affirmed as God's servant
for speaking rightly about Him. These contrasting judgments help us discern what constitutes right and wrong
speech in the context of suffering.

GOOD AND BAD GOD-TALK

How did the friends speak wrongly? Although they
were insensitive, long-winded, hot-tempered, and pre-
sumptuous, they sincerely felt they were speaking on God's
and orthodoxy's behalf. Human beings are constantly guilty
of the indiscretions described above, yet God's anger is such
that there must be something deeper at issue. What kindled
God's wrath? Why must the friends completely humiliate
themselves simply because they served God too zealously?

Conversely, how did Job speak rightly? How could God
approve of Job's speech when He attacked the fundamental
tenets of biblical faith? Consider verse 24:12, where Job
accuses God of indifference over the plight of the wounded

and dying. Verses such as 9:22-24 speak for themselves: "It is all one; therefore I say, he destroys both the blameless and the wicked. When disaster brings sudden death, he mocks at the calamity of the innocent. The earth is given into the hand of the wicked; he covers the eyes of its judge — if it is not he, who then is it?" Why would God prefer Job's lack of orthodoxy to his friends' orthodoxy?

THE NATURE OF TRUE RELIGION: INTEGRITY AND COMPASSION

Quite simply, Job spoke from the heart while the friends spoke from the head. Job pulled no punches. Job thought highly of God, and therefore had great expectations of Him. He was not afraid to confront God with them. Job was a fully human person[47] who believed that he could make certain demands upon God. Although he overstepped the boundaries of the Creator-creature relationship by demanding that God be subject to human laws and expectations, his honesty and integrity kept him open to God's correction.

Whether right or wrong, Job was sincere and gutsy. He was willing to risk everything for what he believed in. He gave God everything he had, holding nothing back. There was no guile in Job.

Conversely, the friends' religious mentality was calculating and retributive. To them, religion was similar to a game with certain rules and procedures. Beliefs were spelled out in undeniable black and white terms, and humanity had to abide by these. These rules and conditions were tolerable as long as you prospered. They wore you down when you suffered.

While the friends gave all the orthodox responses, they

neglected the essential ingredient of mercy, the constant undercurrent of Old Testament faith. Job repeatedly appeals to their sense of mercy and decency. Wasn't there something about Job's plight and appearance that caused them to recoil, rethink their arguments, and retreat into silence? Weren't his troubles such that even religious considerations should be temporarily shelved in the name of compassion?

RETRIBUTION, THE REAL ADVERSARY

Contemplation of Yahweh's judgment of Job and his friends brings us to the story's ultimate villain, retribution doctrine. Lest we think this doctrine is no longer credible, we have only to observe the widespread group and individual violence that plagues the modern world. Underlying most acts of violence is a retributive or retaliatory attitude. Unlike the biblical retribution mentality, we, not God, are the ones charged with executing justice, which inevitably becomes injustice. Even in Jesus' time, retribution doctrine was still widely accepted.[48] Jesus' doctrines of loving one's enemies and of God's indiscriminate goodness reflect His rejection of this perspective on human and divine justice.

Retribution-based self-interest can subtly undermine the religious person's sincere concern with equity and justice. It strips religion of its integrity by reducing human actions to a self-centered barter. We do good because we wish to receive good in return. We avoid evil in fear of punishment. Retribution, unlike reconciliation, does not bring out the best in human beings.

As the wager between God and Satan indicates, in prosperous times it is difficult to determine whether our love and service are rendered unconditionally. When we suffer, our motives become exposed, magnified, and focused. We learn where our treasure lies.

The prologue, dialogues, and epilogue all deal with retribution, and therefore it can rightly be called, in conjunction with its attitudinal alternative, reconciliation, the primary theme of the book.

RECONCILIATION AND SELF-ABANDONMENT: A PRACTICAL ALTERNATIVE

Perhaps the most wonderful aspect of the religious genius of the author of Job is his spiritual practicality. He was not content to discredit the orthodoxy of the time without providing a feasible alternative. In the epilogue we are provided with the central theme of the story and the primary value underlying Job's transformation.

The theme of reconciliation resolves the issues introduced in the prologue in a way challenging to the modern reader and faithful to human values. It is the undercurrent that sheds light on the various relationships that have been developed in the story. Reconciliation, not justice or integrity, is the litmus test of religion. It resolves the various subplots of the story in the following ways:

1. Through communication and reconciliation, the divine-human friendship blossoms.

    In contrast to the heavenly debate, where Yahweh doubted Job enough to permit a wager contesting his purity of motives, Yahweh's communication with Job has left Him confident that Job will offer intercession for his friends. Job was apparently as unaware of God's confidence in the epilogue as he was of His bragging in the prologue. Job is in the dark concerning God's approval of him, just as we often are. This recalls St. Paul's caution

WHERE IS GOD WHEN YOU NEED HIM?

against presuming ourselves to be in a state of grace.⁴⁹ We cannot know the mind or judgments of the Lord. We must simply hold on to our integrity, persist in doing the best we can, and humbly abandon ourselves to God's mercy.

Yahweh's faith in Job signifies the true friendship that has developed through their communications. There is no question in God's mind as to Job's selfless love and obedience. Recall that at this point in the story Job has not been restored to his former status.

2. Job intercedes for his accusers.

Job prays for the very persons who claimed his prayers would not be heard. His role as intercessor is restored, and the issues at hand are no longer imagined (i.e., that Job's children might have cursed God in their hearts) but real (the friends have offended both Job and God).

From a practical, personal growth standpoint, consider how much time and energy is conserved by letting go of resentment towards others and permitting God to be judge and executor of justice.

3. God gratuitously restores Job twofold.

Job's restoration is pursuant to his intercession for his friends. Were Job not to have learned the lesson of reconciliation, his trials would have been for nought. Job's forgiveness of his friends reveals that he no longer conceives of his integrity as a bargaining chip with God or others. This restoration is not to be construed as a quid pro quo reward for Job's goodness. Rather, Yahweh's generosity to Job is in fulfillment of Job's original prayer of faith: "The Lord gave and the Lord has taken away; blessed be the name of the Lord!"⁵⁰

True reconciliation on both the divine-human plane and between human beings is by definition a free response.

God's will for us, which at times leads to joy and at other times suffering, arises out of His freedom and ours. We have the freedom to sin and create crosses for ourselves and others. Our neighbors have the freedom to sin and create crosses for themselves and us. The complex relationships and mysteries involved in suffering clearly place it beyond rational explanation. The friends' inability or unwillingness to recognize this was their fundamental error. All human beings are vulnerable to this temptation to give easy answers.

We can be so quick to fix the blame and interpret the suffering of others as a sign of God's judgment. Life would be much simpler if we worried less about God's motives for rewarding or disciplining others, and instead offered them compassion. By abstaining from judgment on others, we would free ourselves from its yoke as well.[51]

4. Job is comforted by his friends.

Job's need for compassion apparently remains even after his encounter with God and subsequent transformation. This time he is given comforters who are not impeded by the retribution mentality. Note the words of the text: "They showed him sympathy and comforted him for all the evil that the Lord had brought upon him. . ."[52] Those disconcerted by the word 'evil' used in some translations may recall that Hebrew, unlike Latin and Greek, contains no word for suffering. Hence translations often substitute suffering or a similar phrase which conveys the intent of the original.

It is interesting that the text describes his comforters as those who had known him before. Perhaps they experienced a change of heart in concert with Job's transformation. If so, Job's culpability was no longer their business as care-givers. Their job was to comfort, not judge or speculate. Alternatively, they could have viewed Job's restoration as a reward for his repentance in accordance with retribution doctrine. Since Job was now acceptable to God, he was acceptable to them.

The text is silent on the motives of Job's comforters, as if to reflect the issue back on the audience: What are our motivations or justifications for comforting? Do we comfort others out of pity and compassion or out of duty and desire for reward? Is the culpability of the sufferer a factor in our efforts?

5. Job's beautiful daughters receive an inheritance among their brothers.

Job's decision to elevate his daughters to equality with their brothers in the matter of inheritance can be interpreted as another manifestation of his transformation. It is well known that women were severely oppressed in ancient times. This oppression is perceived as a consequence of sin in the book of Genesis,[53] one of the many influences on the book of Job.[54] Perhaps Job's liberation from the retribution mentality has had ripple effects in his already advanced ethical perspective.[55] Uncalculated, gratuitous love, manifested in generosity, is a fruit of Job's new reconciliatory attitude.

6. Job dies old and full of years.

In the wisdom tradition, a long life was both a gift of God and a product of wise living. Although many modern readers are put off by this happier-ever-after ending, in the overall context of biblical faith we can see the wisdom in this conclusion. Although God does permit incomprehensible suffering, and there is indeed much injustice in the world, creation is still good and life remains worth living. We recall the final verse of Job's acceptance speech[56] where he affirms his mistaken perception of the human condition.[57] Job has been able to see the good in life amid great suffering. This theocentric perspective transcends human wisdom and understanding, and must be accepted on faith, as Job has demonstrated. Job's pleasant experience of God's providence is simply an example of the positive side of Job's original statement about God's freedom to give and take away. We must give God room to operate freely, whether the consequences are joyful or painful. In the long run, all things work together for the good of those who love God and are called to Him.[58]

RECONCILIATION AS A FOUNDATION FOR SELF-ESTEEM

The mystery and tragedy of suffering remains unsolved, but God's goodness and justice is understood from a new perspective. The possibility of intimacy and fellowship between creature and Creator endures the most unthinkable of afflictions. Reconciliation is always possible. God desires it even more than we do. He exhorts us to forgive others and accept the imperfections of life without compromising our integrity. The more our self-esteem or self-image is built on the continuing reconciliation of our relationships, with God, ourselves, others, and the material world, the healthier and happier we will be. Unlike modern society, with its sometimes obsessive and functionalistic concern with the self (i.e., you are what you do, and what you think you are), the Bible bases the dignity of the person on their "made in the image of God" status. Our self-image is accurate to the extent that we perceive ourselves and our primary relationships as God does. Healthy self-esteem is within the reach of every individual, for it is dependent on their acceptance of God's perspective, which as Job can attest is quite wonderful. In the next chapter, we will explore God's perspective in more depth by looking at the book of Job as a whole, and parallel themes in the New Testament.

CHAPTER SEVEN

The Lord Takes Away

We will now consider the insights of Job and Jesus into suffering in the context of our personal experience. How can we imitate them in persevering in faith and integrity despite immense suffering? What are the positive attitudes and actions called for by our stories of suffering?

HARD BLESSINGS FOR INNOCENT SUFFERERS

In the prologue Job was stricken in a senseless manner. The narrator's and God's affirmation of his innocence convinces us that there are no skeletons in Job's closet, and therefore his is a classic case of innocent suffering. Innocent suffering is a reality that permeates the Bible, and is displayed most profoundly in the stories of Job and Jesus. In our day, the massive, senseless slaughter of both individuals and peoples through a variety of political, military, and economic scenarios has brought the question of innocent suffering to the foreground. Job and Jesus anticipate these questions, but their response comes in the form of challenging blessings rather than easy answers.

THE QUESTIONS OF SUFFERING

In reaction to his affliction, Job utters parallel phrases that have become a challenge and ideal for sufferers of every period: "The Lord gave and the Lord has taken away; blessed be the name of the Lord!"[59] and "We accept good things from God; should we not accept evil?"[60] It is interesting that the Lord is the subject of the first phrase, while 'we' is the subject of the second phrase. The first phrase is theocentric, and is essentially another way of saying "Your will be done" and "Hallowed be Your name." Note that the Lord's Prayer follows the pattern of Job's statements; the theocentric precedes and provides a context for the anthropocentric.

The challenging words of both Job and Jesus are that for our lives to be properly focused, God's will, whether direct or permissive, must eventually take priority. These are hard words indeed, especially during times of suffering. The rage of Job, as symbolic of our own, demonstrates that this runs counter to human nature. Thus we are faced with the crucial role of prayer: petitioning God for the strength to make our rebellious spirit subject to His will. In our anthropocentric world, this requires a major adjustment of attitude and priorities.

Our prayer pattern is normally the reverse; we start with our personal experience and emotions and work back to God. Amid intense suffering, Job and Jesus began by praying their emotions, and then proceeded to listen for God's word. This pattern is natural and healthy if we gradually progress towards discovery and acceptance of God's will. We begin by expressing ourselves and placing our feelings and disposition before God. Only then can we open ourselves fully to His presence and transcendence.

THE STRUGGLE FOR INTEGRATION

We are challenged by the examples of Job and Jesus to work towards a theocentric perspective in which we place God first in our hearts. The anthropocentric perspective we begin with is necessary, but it must be integrated with the theocentric. This struggle for integration is one of the primary tensions of the spiritual life. Father J.P. de Caussade expressed this well in stating that the practical objective of the spiritual life is seeking and doing the will of God in the present moment. This counsel is particularly relevant during times of suffering, when going beyond the present moment invariably leads to anxiety and depression. So many of our problems and anxieties would resolve themselves if we simply consigned ourselves to the present moment out of trust and obedience to God. Seeking God's will in the present moment is the best we can do for God, ourselves, and others. Fulfilling this simple agenda will require everything our mind, body, and spirit can muster. It is within the capability of every person.

The second phrase, accepting both good and bad at the hand of God, is problematic for the modern humanist. Of course, there are potential misunderstandings, distortions, and disagreements regardless of to whom or to what we attribute suffering. Perhaps we can express Job's question in language less volatile to modern ears, without compromising the truth of the statement: Are we willing to accept life and divine providence in both their joyous and sorrowful dimensions? Are we willing to carry the crosses manifested in both daily and extraordinary trials which are incorporated into God's mysterious plan to save humanity?

Job's questions cited above unknowingly affirm God's admission that He had afflicted Job "for nothing." God ordained a test of Job that seemingly accomplished nothing except to prove His point and destroy Job's (and his family's) world. This test of Job is symbolic of the inexplicable suffering of humanity throughout time. While it may seem to have no earthly merit, it can mysteriously lead to a personal encounter with God and a deeper relationship with not only God, but the world and persons around us. Our suffering can be redemptive for ourselves and others. As discussed in the previous chapter, it can also conform our self-image to God's perspective. Because suffering removes our masks and fronts, it enables us to see ourselves as God sees us, in the naked truth.

While Job's question (i.e., taking the good with the bad) arises from human reason, we intuit from his subsequent outburst that this rational approach is insufficient for coping with such tragedy. Sometimes our suffering is so great that we cannot simply take the bad with the good. We want an explanation from God. We are paralyzed and angered at the thought of meaningless suffering. We shake our fist at God and demand if not an explanation, then at least some meaning. The intercessory nature of Job's and Jesus' suffering reveals that this demand is not only acceptable, but part of God's will. Redemptive suffering is at the heart of the Good News of Job and Jesus. Despite appearances, our suffering is not "for nothing."[61] Because it leads to salvation, it is rather "for everything!"

THE CHALLENGE OF UNCONDITIONAL LOVE

God's wish that we try to love unconditionally is implicit not only in the heavenly debates, but in His personal response to Job. The questions posed by God enlarge Job's vision of human existence and vocation. What more can I do than love someone, including myself and God, simply because they are who they are? To love unconditionally, we will have to see with the eyes of God, which look for and encourage the good in the person. In God's case, we love and obey Him simply because He is God. All rational or emotional motives are secondary, for they will not withstand the crucible of suffering. Before we confidently affirm our loyalty to God and our sisters and brothers, we should recall that the challenge of unconditional love created severe struggles for both Job and Jesus. There is a difficult maturation process that we must undergo before we can affirm this with our hearts. Job blazes this path for us, and we can gain insight from his struggles.

THE SUFFERER'S INTERNAL CONFLICT

Although in spirit Job wished to accept his afflictions, his emotions and nature were of a different mind. He could accept his suffering neither stoically nor piously. He had to speak his mind. It is nice to talk piously of doing God's will, but when it becomes a major cross for us, our human weakness rises to the fore. The path of the cross is through our human nature, and therefore we can expect conflict, confusion, alienation, and rebellion. As Cardinal Carlo Martini, S.J., points out, we can only become ministers of the Gospel when we are so perplexed by it, and it becomes so at odds with our way of doing things, that we discover that it is God's work that we are participating in, and not the reverse. Only when we have been humbled like Job, and consequently tasted the Lord through prayer and contemplation, are we able to attest to God's wisdom, providence, and power, and our own weakness. Prayer and contemplation, both sides of the communication relationship with God, are the pathways through suffering. We are not to look for answers, but to place ourselves as we are, complaints and all, in the presence of God. Contrary to the skepticism of certain religious and secular critics, getting angry at God can be a power for good if we let God transform our anger into actions and attitudes in conformity with His will. We can be passionate both towards and for God amidst our personal experience of suffering.

SERMON ON THE DUMP

It is interesting that God restored Job subsequent to his intercession for his friends. God loved Job's friends, and it was apparently important to God that Job love his friends as well. The prologue had raised the question of human motives, and Job had vindicated Yahweh's faith in the unconditional nature of Job's love for both God and his fellow human beings. In this reconciliatory act, Job anticipates the radical demands of the Sermon on the Mount. In Mt 5:48, Jesus asks that His followers be perfect as His Father is perfect,[62] which they will achieve by loving indiscriminately. Note the similar challenges of Jesus' words concerning the need to pray for one's persecutors and Job's intercessory mission as explained in Job 42:7-9. In light of Jesus' call to wholeness, it is perplexing that Christians interested in personal growth frequently turn to secular avenues without considering the Christian resources available, pre-eminent of which is the Bible.

We might also recall that the narrator begins Job's opening speech (chapter 3) with the same words (and he opened his mouth . . .) that preface the Matthean Beatitudes. In a mystical, existential sense, we could read Job's speeches as our initial human response to the divine demands of the Sermon on the Mount.

If we try to live out the Sermon, we will invariably suffer unjustly and experience the miseries deemed cause for happiness by Jesus.[63] In our human weakness, we struggle with the call to unconditional love and service. We require some outlet or sounding board. While God can inspire and support us through prayer, contemplation, and His mysterious initiative and providence, we also need our family, friends, and the Christian community to help us in practical ways through listening, understanding, counsel, and compassion. Because (like Job's friends) these human support systems will at times disappoint us as we try to live out the values and demands of the Sermon on the Mount, it will be helpful to have the Sermon on the Dump for reference as a model for expressing our pain to God. Job's fiery and penetrating speeches can serve as an inspiration and starting point in communicating our feelings to God.

REDEMPTIVE SUFFERING

The suffering that Job experienced as part of his crash course in unconditional love was redemptive for the most unlikely characters, his religious friends. This anticipates a mysterious and glorious aspect of the Christian vocation of suffering: its redemptive nature. Our obedience to God's will when it contradicts ours unites us to the crucified Jesus who shared our cataclysmic struggle with human nature. We then fulfill the words of St. Paul, who spoke of our suffering as completing the afflictions of Christ.[64] We live the paschal mystery when we love amidst suffering, and reconcile without motive. We become the unsung heroes of the Gospel, the anonymous just who quietly minister to Christ in the person of the human sufferer.[65]

THE CLASHING OF HUMAN AND DIVINE FREEDOM

In Job's final testimony, chapters 29-31, he spoke of the many manifestations of his virtues, chief of which was his care for the forgotten and oppressed. It is interesting that in his spiritual classic *Morals on the Book of Job*, St. Gregory the Great remarks that Yahweh disciplines Job in order to protect him from pride and a sense of self-sufficiency. Lest his actions spring from self-aggrandizement and pride in religious observance, rather than love, the Lord spoke to Job and revealed the radical freedom on the part of both God and humanity that is characteristic of true religion. The conclusion of Job's final speech, in which he describes himself as a prince and defiantly signs his complaint, reveals that he felt his suffering entitled him to some explanation or recompense from God. We feel the same way when we suffer.

The tough-to-swallow response from God is that there are mutual freedoms and personal integrities involved that preclude Job from making such insistent claims on God. Job can get mad at God all he wants as long as he recognizes God's rights as God. God respects our human freedom to question and grouse at Him, as well as to commit sins or do good. Conversely, He expects us to respect His integrity as

Creator, Provider, Redeemer, and Judge. We may not like the way He does His job, but we must respect His rights as God. He is bound neither by human justice nor religious laws and traditions. Religion must leave room for God to be God, as each individual needs room to be themselves. That is why Job's statements in the prologue about the Lord's giving and taking, and the complementary human response of blessing God and accepting His will are critical; we need to adopt God's perspective through free human assent and obedience. This challenging process of integration will be with us throughout our time on earth.

Like any relationship, the divine-human one is worked out through faith, trust, communication, and love. These require hard work, and inevitably involve suffering. The catalyzing and climactic role of prayer in Job is therefore not surprising. The story begins and ends with Job offering intercession. This recalls the redemptive potential of suffering mentioned earlier: Through the power of God, our stripes can heal others as well as ourselves.

THE FREEDOM OF LOVE

Because the most liberating response a human being can make is love, let us consider the simple words of 1 Corinthians 13. Note the spirit of freedom implicit in each adjective used to describe love. These are an exhortation for those parts of ourselves that have the attitude of Job's religious friends. Job's friends could have used this passage to put their role in perspective. These words serve as a code of behavior for the care-giver. They are a charter and guide for the believer who is serious about the Lord's call to unconditional love. They are beautiful but impossible ideals until we invite the Lord to guide and sustain us in living them out.

GOD'S WAYS ARE NOT OURS

The ways in which the Lord executes His divine plan and justice are certainly different than we would have it. We emulate Job in desiring a retributive God who wields the divine ax and weeds out the wicked according to human standards of justice. Not coincidentally, He vindicates and rewards us in the process. Jesus cautions the Church against such a retributive attitude in the parable of the wheat and the tares.[66] Both the Church and the individual Christian should be wary of usurping God's role as judge. We may not always realize it, but we are fortunate that God operates this way, for if God did execute justice according to our standards, we would undoubtedly condemn ourselves.[67]

CHAPTER EIGHT

The Lord Gives

One of the common traits of saints, living and dead, is their progressive affirmation of Job's platitude: "The Lord gives and the Lord takes away." We know how difficult it is to accept the Lord's privilege to take away, even if it is for our good. Paralleling this difficulty is our similar indigestion with attributing all good things to God. It is necessary to accept both sides of Job's proposition. While in modern times the tendency is to reject God's permissive involvement in suffering (i.e. the taking away aspect), there also exists the danger that we will become de-sensitized to the many ways that the Lord gives. Reflection on the giving and restoring activity of God in our lives is as important as contemplation of His taking away. If we don't integrate and balance the two, we may not only become depressed and cynical, but we will fail to recognize the blessings God grants to us.

These blessings are not always readily apparent. Sometimes they can only be discerned when we conform our life vision to God's. Throughout the Scriptures, God is perceived in seemingly inconsequential events as much as in grand ones. In our sensationalist times, we have been pro-grammed to revere the big score, the grand catch, the over-whelming success. We are losing the consciousness that enables us to see God in quiet, humble realities.

The divine Giver gives freely according to His own agenda. We prefer our human gifts given and received with a similar sense of freedom. We are free to overlook or reject His gifts. We often reject the gifts God gives us because they are not what we want or think we need. It is tempting for us to make demands on the giver or to take their gifts for granted. This is especially true when the giver is God, who gives in quiet and subtle, as well as extraordinary, ways. Unlike most human givers, He is less concerned with pleas-ing us than in helping us even if He incurs our anger in the process. Sometimes the greatest gifts that God bestows on us are the most challenging. Gifts that call us to more loving and faithful relationships can be difficult to receive.

KNOWING HOW TO RECEIVE

What if our story had ended with Job refusing to accept God's restoration, saying he was undeserving of it, or that God was simply setting him up for another fall? Because Job had accepted His message of mutual freedom and integrity, God knew he would recognize his restoration as a gift rather than a reward in fulfillment of retribution principles. This is not to say that God does not reward us, or that we should not desire a reward. On the contrary, the book of Hebrews states that a desire for reward is one of the prerequisites of faith.[68] According to Jesus (e.g., the Beatitudes), our de-sires should be centered on heavenly rewards, the first fruits of which we experience on earth. For Jesus, earthly happi-ness derives from contemplation of the heavenly values and rewards anticipated by believers. The kingdom of God is not of this world. Accordingly, neither should we expect to find our true treasure here.

This is quite a different message from the one promoted by our materialist culture. Some of our psycho-spiritual suffering emanates from the false expectations programmed into us by the self-seeking culture we live in. One of the reasons we immerse ourselves in Christian culture[69] is to gradually liberate ourselves, by grace, from the snares of the world. The interior freedom underlying this liberation propels us towards our human potential and Christian vocation.

GOD, THE SOURCE OF ALL GOODNESS

When we deny that the Lord takes away through His permissive (as opposed to direct) will, perhaps attributing it to random and arbitrary forces, it is possible that unconsciously we may feel that these gifts are not His to take away. We lose sight of the fact that all good things proceed from God,[70] and are His to distribute as He pleases.[71] We act as if our efforts to procure these gifts are unaided and uninspired. Perhaps in some cases they are, such as when we seek what God does not will for us. Even then, the Lord rains and shines on the just and unjust.[72]

The American ethic of self-reliance is a great danger for Christians to the extent that we feel we earn or deserve all the good that happens to us. It is true that we work for things and according to legitimate principles of human justice we deserve some reward. This does not diminish the fact that we remain indebted to the Lord. Even those gifts we receive through our efforts are ours on loan. If we can work hard to earn something, who gave us the ability, strength, and opportunity? It is true that we cooperate with God in this, and that without both parties' involvement the transaction would be adversely affected. It is when we feel entitled to certain things from God that problems arise.

Even if we believe that He wills our ultimate good, it is difficult for us to view such basics as our health, loved ones, and life's necessities as gifts, and therefore at God's disposal to give or permit to be taken away. For the Christian, all things must contain the clause, "If God wills." When we struggle with the call to subordinate our needs and desires to God's will, we can imitate Job in entering into a sincere and perhaps passionate dialogue with God.

All communication functions better when things are out in the open. The advantage of communication with God is that we don't have to be sensitive to His feelings or anxious about our timing. God loves us infinitely. He is glad whenever we go to Him, even if on our own stubborn terms. It is easier for Him to work on our hearts when we are engaged in dialogue with Him, whether during daily quiet time or amid our daily activities, than when we pout and ignore Him.

THE LOST VALUE OF DISCIPLINE

Parallel to our blindness to the source of our gifts is our diminished awareness of God's involvement in our lives in a disciplinary fashion. We fail to recognize that God's removal of His gifts can be a manifestation of His discipline. He may be trying to teach us something. Perhaps we have distorted a value that He chooses to correct through this particular action. Because we never know with certainty the mind of God, we simply proceed in faith and accept reality as it comes to us, striving to work with it as best we can.

The book of Hebrews provides us with an excellent analogy, stressing that if our earthly parents discipline us for our good, how much more will the discipline of our heavenly Father work to our advantage.[73] The author of Hebrews is very realistic in recognizing that all discipline at time of application is an occasion for sorrow. Obedience and fidelity doesn't imply that we enjoy God's methods. We are not made to enjoy suffering, however beneficial it may be in the long run. We are called to pursue and fulfill God's will amidst our suffering, while turning to God for sustenance and redemption.

CHOOSING TO SEE THE GOOD

Ultimately, acknowledgment of the gratuitous nature of life is a matter of perception. This awareness must come from the heart of the individual, in the biblical sense of the whole person. One of the amazing realities of life is that persons who on the surface would seem to have little reason to thank God, e.g., the poor, the sick, the disabled, etc., are often the most lavish, faithful, and sincere in their praise of Him. Conversely, those with an abundance of earthly blessings often choose to focus on the things they don't have. This is partially due to cultural consumerist programming, in which the objective of life is to accumulate as much as we can for as little outlay as possible.

When we are convinced that we know what is best for us, we are likely to overlook the gifts God gives us on a daily basis. The process of awakening ourselves to God's gifts will take a lifetime, but it is potential-fulfilling, manageable, and healthy. Until we learn to recognize and thank God for the gifts He gives, however small to our eyes, we will not respect His freedom to take away.

Part of the problem is our unwillingness to be satisfied with the earthly and spiritual bread that comes from heaven. We don't comprehend Jesus' quotation of Deuteronomy 6:16 in response to the temptations of Satan: "One does not live by bread alone, but by every word that comes forth from the mouth of God."[74] Do we really believe that all of life proceeds from and is sustained by God's word? Our anthropocentric life vision has diminished our awareness of the hidden heavenly source of the earthly blessings we so often take for granted.

If we view this bread apart from its source, we will develop unhealthy attachments to God's material gifts. In the Lord's Prayer, Jesus instructs us to ask for our daily bread,[75] not for what is unnecessary and luxurious. The challenge of Job and Jesus extends far beyond a simple change of attitude or perspective. Acceptance of these challenging but fulfilling directives entails a transformation and reorientation of the whole person, body, mind, and spirit. The practice of *lectio divina* can facilitate this transformation.

HUMILITY AND INTERIOR DETACHMENT: THE NECESSARY INGREDIENTS

Humility is a key factor in our recognition of both ends of Job's proposition. We must be humble to acknowledge that God knows what our daily bread is, even when our senses disagree, and that those things we don't currently perceive as gifts are also gifts. We may discover their value over time, or they may remain a mystery to us. Acknowledging all of life as gift is itself a gift of faith. When we see the transitory nature of our possession and experience of earthly realities, and the growth and redemptive opportunities inherent in the Lord's giving and taking, it is easier to let go of them.

As St. Paul says, what do we have that we did not receive? When we let go of our possessive claim on things, even our health, basic needs, and our loved ones, we free ourselves to receive the greatest gift of all — God. Correspondingly, we give God and ourselves room to give and receive these gifts in compliance with His wisdom and will. When we receive them in a spirit of freedom, we appreciate them more, and our perspective on these gifts is grounded in truth.

This interior detachment was the gift Job received that enabled him to change his mind about the deplorable condition of human existence, and revoke his law suit against God. We can see that Job's statement of faith in 1:21 covers much more than his or our reaction to loss; it entails a whole way of looking at life. His is a way of reconciling oneself to life by obediently seeking redeeming values in the present moment and situation, rather than continually fighting life and ending up in bitterness and despair.

SUFFERING: AN OPPORTUNITY FOR MERCY AND INTEGRITY

The guiding life principle of the book of Job and the Christian faith is that all of life is gift and grace. Nothing we do entitles us to anything from God. That He will reward and even praise us is His free gift. Because of our pride and possessiveness, and the influence of the anthropocentric world we live in, this can be hard to accept.

When we look at God's exercise of freedom from an objective standpoint, we have reason to praise Him for His generosity and mercy. Were we in God's position, we would doubtless not treat our servants as well as God treats us. Thank God that His justice is not ours. A world governed by strict retribution would be horrible. Life would be nothing but mechanical payback. Such a world is as inconceivable as a world without any form of justice.

When we suffer, we discover ways in which we inflict suffering on others. Suffering becomes an opportunity to petition God's mercy for ourselves as well as for others, while deepening our personal integrity through a resolve to avoid this sin in the future. His mercy is the gift that frees us to forgive others and be reconciled with them.

When we discover how much it hurts when others injure us, or vice-versa, the Holy Spirit and our conscience compel us to live a more sincere and honest life in business and at home, as well as at church. Can people see our Christian faith in the way we do business or treat our loved ones? Do we do business by the principle of retribution: Treat others with courtesy and respect as long as you have something to gain from them? One barometer of our business integrity is how we treat salespersons or merchants from whom we do not intend to purchase anything. If we are rude, manipulative, or misleading, it is Christ we are mistreating. The marketplace and home, like the church parking lot, is the acid test of the Christian faith.

An important aspect of integrity is simply standing by our word. When we give our word to people, do we intend on following through? The words of Jesus on the matter of pronouncing oaths: "Let your 'Yes' mean 'Yes' and your 'No' mean 'No.' Anything more is from the evil one"[76] are a beacon of truth for our superficial and excessively pragmatic culture.

Once again we see a distinction between Christian and secular perspectives on human development. For many secular personal growth proponents, integrity is only a means to an end, a path bounded by reasonableness and reward.[77] For the Christian, integrity is something worth suffering or even dying for. Job's willingness to die for his integrity impressed God enough that He made an appearance. When we view our integrity in the context of the four basic relationships[78] we perceive it not as a luxury but as a sacred gift and responsibility.

Though Job was confronted and rebuked by God, he emerged unscathed. He had previously doubted God's willingness to listen to Him.[79] Overwhelmed by God's mercy and transcendence, the transformed Job is able to extend that mercy to his accusers. If we are to follow in Job's reconciliatory footsteps, we must recognize both the presence of and our need for God's mercy in daily life.

PASTORAL CAUTION

Before we try to convince others of these perspectives, we must convince ourselves. Self-abandonment to divine providence is easy to affirm when the Lord gives, but is quite difficult when He takes away. Human nature finds it difficult to accept the Lord's taking away, including acknowledging that He has the right or power to take away.

Many people long for some experience of God's love, whether through direct encounter or as mediated by the love of other persons. How can we expect persons to affirm Job's statement when they have never truly tasted the Lord's giving? In situations where we are tempted to be harsh and judgmental, it is important to remember that the work of evangelization is ultimately God's. We can only cooperate by becoming persons of peace, understanding, and reconciliation.

SUFFERING'S CALL FOR NAKED FAITH AND UNCONDITIONAL LOVE

As emphasized throughout this book, we may never understand why the Lord takes away in certain instances. It ultimately becomes a question of unconditional love and what at least feels like naked faith. At times we feel like Abraham and Isaac, asked to return our most treasured possession, be it our loved one or life itself.[80] The God of the Promise is also the God of the Call.

JOB AS A SYMBOL OF THE REDEEMER

St. Gregory the Great spends approximately one-third of his commentary on Job discussing the allegorical sense of Scripture, in which he treats Job as a symbol of Jesus. Along with a plethora of subsequent saints, St. Gregory relates the trials and words of Job to those of Christ. The way of Job is the way of the Cross. The paschal mystery is the Christian's ultimate destination, and Job is a practical guide to the many struggles and temptations we will experience along this path. These include bad comforters, denial, anger, depression, bargaining, fear, resentment, defiance, physical illness, and a sense of alienation from God, our body, the community, and even our family. Job learned to cope with this suffering through prayer, contemplation, and reconciliation.

Jesus embellishes Job, for He is the Word made flesh. The personified Wisdom in the Wisdom Poem is superceded by the ultimate incarnation of divine wisdom, Jesus Christ. The revelation of the whirlwind is surpassed by the revelation of Calvary. Christ's seven 'words' from the cross transcend the Yahweh Speeches as a personal revelation on suffering. Job's earthly restoration is superseded by our eternal restoration through Christ's resurrection, which according to John's Gospel becomes a present reality for believers. The elegance of Job's daughters is paralleled by the beauty of the church, of whom Mary is a symbol.

In a world plagued by widespread oppression of women, especially the economically and socially vulnerable, it is essential that we turn to the mother of Jesus for inspiration, guidance, and consolation. In the next chapter, we will look at the woman who embodied, to the fullest degree, the self-abandonment to divine providence to which Job aspired.

CHAPTER NINE

New Testament Models

THE NEED FOR HUMAN MODELS
OF FAITHFULNESS AND HOPE

Sometimes the pure faith and obedience of Jesus during the passion is difficult for us to relate to, and we get discouraged. Mary complements Job as a model of contemplation, self-abandonment, and hope for beleaguered sufferers. In her faithful response to the word of God, she is a model of human potential and vocation. As discussed in Cardinal Carlo Martini's *Women and Reconciliation*, she demonstrates the feminine virtues of attentiveness, practicality, listening, celebration, tenderness, and giving.

MARY, MOTHER AND SISTER IN SUFFERING

Mary is mother, sister, and inspiration to those who endeavor to accept both good and bad at the hand of providence. If we are going to work through suffering in

Christian solidarity, Mary's attitude and life can inspire us. We can relate to the down-to-earth Mary whom a sword pierced[81] as she followed Jesus to the cross,[82] and who at times seemed confused by Jesus,[83] yet had great faith in Him.[84] Her "*fiat*"[85] disposition led her into all types of situations in which suffering was present, either her own or others'. The anguished cry of the mother of God, witnessing her only Son's execution, is capable of melting human hearts and bringing people in pain together. If our hearts are not stirred at the passionate cry of the human mother, be she Mary at the cross, Job's wife, or the many suffering mothers and would-be mothers in our midst, then we will not likely hear the cry of her Son in the suffering persons we meet every day.[86]

MARY, SPIRITUAL COUSIN TO JOB

The Scriptures testify that Mary embraced the painful but joyful way of the cross. In the New Testament accounts in which Mary is mentioned, we find the themes of suffering, discipleship, and glory that accompany the cross.

Just as Job held on to his hope that God would vindicate him, despite apparent rejection, Mary had confidence in the goodness of Jesus, even when He seemed to rebuff her, as at the wedding at Cana.[87] Job's and Mary's persistent faith amidst confusion and negative circumstances are an example for us when we suffer and perceive ourselves to be neglected by God. God confounded Job's and Mary's expectations just as He does ours. If Mary and Job, two whole and holy individuals, have imperfect expectations of God, shall we be surprised when we miss the mark?

A BLESSING INSTEAD OF A CURSE

In the life of Mary we see the most profound meaning of the phrase "the Lord gives and the Lord takes away." Her *fiat* epitomizes her acceptance of this principle. The Magnificat[88] is essentially a fleshing out of Job's "Blessed be the name of the Lord."

Whereas Job's faith in God's providence and initiative in human events led him to a personal encounter with the transcendent Yahweh, Mary's faith in providence brought her to a different sort of summit, a painful encounter with the crucified Lord at the foot of the cross. Her response of faithfulness amidst anguish stands in direct contrast to the despair of Job's wife. At her personal Gethsemane, she attached her *fiat* to Jesus' "Thy will be done."

Jesus was God's gift to Mary, but God asked her, like Abraham, to let go of her beloved Son, not just at Calvary, but at Cana and en route from Jerusalem.[89] It was at the moment of Mary's greatest trial, her greatest experience of God's taking away, that she received her greatest gift in the beloved disciple. Mary would remain the mother of Jesus, but now her motherhood would extend to all of Jesus' brothers and sisters, as symbolized by the beloved disciple.[90] Like the beloved disciple, we can turn to her for inspiration and consolation as we struggle to bless God rather than curse Him when we are put to the test.

In her humble trust and obedience, Mary is a living model of self-abandonment to divine providence. By suffering in solidarity, we await with Mary and Job and the rest of our brothers and sisters our vindication and consolation at the foot of the cross. Let us now examine the "*fiat*" prayer par excellence, the Lord's Prayer.

THE LORD'S PRAYER: PRAYER OF THE SUFFERING CHRISTIAN

Because we have been dealing with the mystery of suffering and the process of God's perfection of His creatures, it is only appropriate that we conclude our reflections with a reference to the perfect prayer. We pray this prayer in light of the prayer of Jesus in Gethsemane, especially as reported by the evangelists Luke and Matthew.[91]

The petitions in the Lord's Prayer are intrinsically connected with human suffering. Each reveals an attitude the believer strives to have towards God, neighbor, the material world, or the self. As previously mentioned, Job anticipates the Lord's Prayer in his blessing of God's name and his willingness to forgive and seek forgiveness. The testing of Job by Yahweh brings to mind the second to last petition of the Lord's Prayer, "Do not subject us to the test."

Being Put To The Test

The last verse of the Lord's Prayer in Luke's Gospel has traditionally been rendered, "and lead us not into temptation." The Greek word *peirasmos*, translated as temptation, may more appropriately be rendered as test, for reasons explained in Fr. La Verdiere's study.[92] *Peirasmos* does not imply a moral or psychological temptation as much as a cataclysmic trial in which the individual's entire vocation and faith is tested. In Gethsemane, Jesus twice tells His apostles to petition God to spare them from the test. Jesus was aware of the sting of this ultimate test, mysteriously permitted by God. In the Lord's Prayer, He soberly warns His disciples to pray that (subject to God's will) they be spared it.

The words of Jesus in Gethsemane are food for reflection in the context of human suffering. The suffering we experience may cause us to feel like we are being given this supreme test or passion experience. The sleepiness of the apostles in Gethsemane and their desertion of Jesus amidst His trial epitomize the natural response of human beings to intense suffering. The spirit is willing but human nature is weak. We simply cannot endure the test of suffering by ourselves. All of us have vulnerabilities and breaking points. In certain situations, but for the grace of God, we would undoubtedly crack.

Manifestations of this cataclysmic test in the modern world include victims of violence, the physically or mentally disabled, persons suffering the harsh effects of aging, the unemployed and underemployed, victims of tragic accidents, and persons impeded from fulfilling their vocation in various ways. Realities such as these aptly capture the sense of *peirasmos*. When we undergo these trials, our entire calling and vision of life are tested. This is the temptation of meaninglessness and despair that is so prevalent today.

If we are being tested either as sufferer or care-giver, we can ask what the word of God can do for us in these circumstances. We will need to find God in our everyday experiences which on the surface appear meaningless. If we are to discover God's initiative in our lives, we will need to become everyday contemplatives. How do we find God when He gives and when He takes away?

While the path for each person is unique, we can draw on both Job and the Christian mystical tradition for some down-to-earth wisdom. In the next chapter, we will consider the answer Job received to the question he articulated on behalf of sufferers of all times: Where is God when you need Him?

CHAPTER TEN

Job: Model Of Everyday Mysticism

To cope with the mysteries of life, especially suffering, one must understand its language and symbols. A Christian mystic enters into these mysteries in search of God and truth. Job is an everyday mystic because in his unceasing quest for God he discovers that all of life is a mystery. His final words[93] reveal his joy over the discovery of an intimate, personal relationship with God. Mysticism is the journey from hear-say religion to personal encounter with God in the present moment. Job's spiritual journey resembles a grand symphony in which diverse notes, instruments, and tempos are mysteriously integrated to form a moving concerto. Let us observe the elements and movements of Job's spirituality as inspiration for discovering God's involvement and call in our own life.

We can outline the broad patterns of Job's spiritual journey using the language of the Christian contemplative tradition. For our purposes, this need not be complex and philosophical. Those wishing to delve deeper into mysticism can consult the works discussed at the conclusion of the chapter.

Job dramatizes the two Christian contemplative paths traditionally known as the *apophatic* and the *kataphatic*. These complementary streams describe how believers discover and experience God at various moments and stages of their life. Both are necessary for a balanced prayer and active life.

Job illustrates the need for a balanced, integrated spirituality when he speaks of receiving both good and bad from the hand of God. Believers need to be able to find God and hope in all situations. Life is composed of experiences ranging the spectrum from joy and friendship to despair and alienation. Job, whose life spanned both poles, provides inspiration and dynamic images rather than instructions on the art of responding both to God's presence and absence as manifested in our life experiences. The path he discovers for getting through his suffering integrates the human experience of God's presence and absence in a practical way suitable for appropriation by believers of all eras.

THE KATAPHATIC OR POSITIVE PATH (IN LATIN, VIA AFFIRMATIVA)

The positive contemplative stream, known in mystical theology as kataphatic, approaches God from the incarnational perspective. In the kataphatic stream, we experience God as present. The mystery of the Word made flesh inspires the believer's openness to seeing God in all of creation. Kataphatic contemplation derives its inspiration from the positive ways God reveals Himself. We intuit God's presence in nature, persons, and the everyday events in life through our senses, faith, and reason. In Job, this tradition of contemplation is anticipated by the Yahweh Speeches, where Job is invited to contemplate nature, the wicked, his own ignorance and impotence, and the beasts of chaos from God's vantage point. When he accepts this invitation, he experiences a change of mind and heart. By integrating the senses with faith and reason, Job discovers the mysterious activity and presence of God in the world. This gift of contemplation or 'seeing rightly' was a manifestation of grace, coming as it did through the divine revelation. However, Job freely participated in this revelation through his attentive listening and pliant spirit.

That Job experienced God in positive, incarnational events is evident in his refined ability to celebrate. The book of Job begins and ends with feasting. Job's intercession for his children in verses 1:4-5 reveals his consciousness of God's presence at their meal, thus calling for reverent human behavior. When we celebrate, do we see God as inspiration or participant in our joy? What part does He play in our experience of life's good times?

What does this mean on a practical level? Simply that our faith must contain an active incarnational element. We must be open to the initiative and presence of God in human affairs on both a personal and community level. This can be as simple as recording in a personal journal our experience of God's initiative in our life. We can pray our feelings by sharing with God either vocally or in writing the different ways in which we experienced either His presence or absence during the course of our day. How did God reveal Himself? How were my experiences touched by God's presence, whether in nature, other persons, or through specific events? Perhaps God spoke to me through a smile, a chance meeting, a pretty flower, or a quiet sunset. That God can be perceived from creation has been continually affirmed by the Church, beginning with St. Paul.[94] The beautiful creation stories in Genesis testify to the Jewish awareness of God's presence in creation.

DISCOVERING GOD'S PRESENCE IN LIFE

Joy, wonder, peace, wholeness, and humor are dispositions that mark the kataphatic path. These are graces that flow from our discovery of God's presence in our lives and in the world. As Christians we believe that the incarnation, together with the paschal mystery, has put creation as well as humanity on the road to redemption.[95] With the eyes of faith and a spirit of discernment, we seek God's will and rejoice when we experience His mysterious presence, not just in major events, but in everyday, seemingly inconsequential realities as well.

THE APOPHATIC OR NEGATIVE PATH (IN LATIN, VIA NEGATIVA)

Perhaps the two best words, taken together, to describe the apophatic way of contemplation are the New Testament Greek term *kenosis*, and the Spanish term *nada*, used by St. John of the Cross. *Kenosis* refers to the humble emptying and submission of the Crucified Jesus. Its meaning is beautifully articulated in the early Christian hymn found in Philippians 2:1-11. *Nada* as used by St. John simply means "nothing." He uses it in reference to the absoluteness of God. According to St. John, Christians must be single-minded and progressively free of attachments in their love and service of God and neighbor. Nothing must come in the way of their pursuit of His will and word. This is an underlying theme of Yahweh's message to Job. Not even Job's extreme suffering and stress limits God's freedom to act as He sees fit. Everything received from God is gift and grace.

Lest we get discouraged, we must recall that even such holy individuals as Job and St. John struggled with incorporating *nada* in their life vision. The apophatic way describes the process of emptying ourselves before God in recognition of our status as creatures.

The apophatic way recognizes, in concert with St. Thomas Aquinas, that it is more theologically correct to say what God is not, than what He is. This compels us to let go of our tendency to box God in and subject Him to narrow and rigid human prescriptions. Whereas in the kataphatic stream, we relate to God through our experience of His presence, in the apophatic we discover Him both in our experience of His absence and in our emptying before Him. Our five senses are primarily receptive during apophatic contemplation, whereas they are more active during kataphatic contemplation (e.g., when we experience God in a tree). In apophatic contemplation, we recognize the limitations of our theological concepts and our sensory efforts to perceive God. We just let ourselves 'be' before God, and attempt to empty ourselves of those things, sensory, rational, or material, that hinder us from experiencing His presence.

In the apophatic way, we grow in intimacy with God through a process of 'unknowing.' We permit God to reveal Himself to us by letting go of those things which impede His communication. Sometimes, as when we suffer, we have no choice but to let certain things go. When we hold on to them we make our situation worse. How we react to our loss will determine whether we open ourselves enough to let God fill our void in His own way.

Times of disorder and chaos (e.g., suffering and stress) are especially amenable to apophatic contemplation. When we grieve the loss of something good, we recognize our nakedness before God. It then becomes easier to come to Him free of distracting encumbrances. When we suffer, it is more commonly our experience that we are abandoned by God than that He is all around us. This was Job's experience, and it led Him to a profound and graced synthesis of the kataphatic and apophatic streams. In order to develop a balanced spirituality, we must accustom ourselves to experiences and periods of God's (perceived) absence as well as His presence. It may be helpful to consider Job's path to apophatic contemplation as a general guide to our own.

JOB AND THE APOPHATIC PATH

Most of the book of Job is spent articulating and refuting the cry of Job. Job describes his condition through an array of earthy images and pregnant phrases that invite the reader to take a stance on the meaning of life, justice, and religion in light of suffering. The common denominator of his lamentations is the theme of darkness and futility. Job speaks of God hemming him in or hiding his way.[96] He can neither see where he is going nor do anything about his situation. Perhaps the most profound description of Job's experience is provided by St. John of the Cross, who terms such desolation "the dark night of the soul." This is the path of the cross, of interior aridity and spiritual desolation.

The glorious anthropology of Psalm 8 and the incarnational theology of Psalm 139 are directly contradicted by Job.[97] To understand the truth of these Psalms, Job will need to go beyond superficial human experience. Hearsay support for these and other religious truths will not stand the test of suffering. Job needs to personally experience the goodness of God and creation through contemplation and Yahweh's revelation.

Job, like the rest of Scripture, does not conceal the unpleasant and paradoxical elements of reality. While he does not provide a solution to life's problems and tragedies, he does blaze a path for getting through them with God. The word of God does not take away the mystery of life; it simply reveals the even greater mystery of God which must be taken on faith, hope, and love.

Job gives us hope whenever the word of God rings hollow in our hearts. Along with the seemingly abandoned Jesus on the cross, he stands as the biblical model par excellence of the human experience of God's absence. The paradox of Job is that, at the moment religious orthodoxy failed him, this missing God came to his rescue.

WHEN YOU LEAST EXPECT HIM...

Job's persistent desire for divine justice apparently compelled God to pay him a visit. The circumstances that would seem to dictate God's absence instead lead to His presence. During his suffering, Job knew God as the one who is both absent and obstructive. His experience of God's total incomprehensibility and elusiveness results in the destruction of Job's tidy retribution-based image of God. In the silent, contemplative posture before God that followed his laments,[98] Job's stillness gives God room to reveal Himself not only in incarnational ways (e.g., through nature), but through Job's experience of *nada*. In true apophatic fashion, Job came to know God first hand by being known by Him, and by acknowledging that he was ignorant in divine matters.

In the apophatic stream, we discover God when we admit we don't know the way. We thus dispose ourselves for God's gratuitous revelation. Through the apophatic path of unknowing, Job is stripped down in order to be built up. Although the author never explicitly states this, we can postulate that Job's *nada* experience helped him discover his latent pride and presumption, which would have greatly obstructed the kataphatic vision of life that Yahweh offered from the whirlwind. In Job, the two paths of contemplation flow together in a type of spiritual dialogue. They catalyze and refine each other. The apophatic path purifies us of the extra baggage we receive on the kataphatic journey. The kataphatic path strengthens and stabilizes us for the self-emptying aspect of the apophatic experience.

SUFFERING, CONTEMPLATION, AND LECTIO DIVINA

By reading, meditating upon, praying, and contemplating the speeches of Job in *lectio divina*, we can enter into the deep regions of the human spirit. There we find our most powerful and vulnerable feelings towards God, life, ourselves, and others. Reflection on the words of Job brings us to the core of what it means to be a human being in the midst of suffering. In *lectio divina* we bring our personal experience of both God's presence and absence to the word of God. We let Job's inspired words shed light on our situation. We can claim, reject, or modify his words, depending on our feelings and experience. Job's insights into both apophatic and kataphatic contemplation help us relate *lectio divina* to everyday life.

DAILY OPPORTUNITIES FOR APOPHATIC CONTEMPLATION

Job took the preposterous risk (just ask the friends who deemed him arrogant and crazy) of requesting a direct audience with God (his pleas for an arbiter apparently falling on deaf ears), and was miraculously rewarded. The darkness which enclosed Job did not deter either Job or God from the communication process. Instead, it gave Job time to empty himself of religious doctrines that caused him to conceive of God as adversary rather than friend.

The saints continually speak of God's desire to be desired by us. Imperfect desires and mixed motives are no excuse for remaining passive. When we experience God's absence, let us follow the example of Job, the persistent widow,[99] the Canaanite woman,[100] the good thief,[101] and the many other anonymous heroes of the Gospels in pursuing God despite darkness and foreboding circumstances. Use this period of aridity to discover who and what God is not, as well as who or what He is. Make it a practice to empty yourself of thoughts, emotions, and concepts before God on a daily basis. The centering prayer method discussed below and the awareness exercises proposed by Anthony de Mello, S.J., are excellent instruments for inducing apophatic contemplation. Many of Fr. de Mello's exercises are helpful in stimulating kataphatic contemplation as well.

THE NEED FOR DISCERNMENT

Job's insights into discernment are primarily at the level of prayer. He doesn't repress his feelings and experiences when speaking of his pain. He is willing to listen when God talks. Following Job, when our speaking, listening, and prayer gets to the gut-level, we can more confidently trust the insights we receive.

The ambiguities of the spiritual and active life necessitate that we take seriously the practice of discernment. How do we discern whether the impulses, intuitions, and insights we experience during silent or active contemplation are from God, the devil, or neither? Prayer groups, Bible studies, and other Church-related support groups inject objectivity, group discernment, and practical and spiritual wisdom into our growth path. The ideal is individual or group spiritual direction, but such opportunities are rare, especially for lay persons. Because discernment is so essential to the contemplative lifestyle, it is recommended that readers familiarize themselves with the Ignatian method, hopefully under the direction of a spiritual guide. The works of the authors listed below are especially helpful, though they are no substitute for one-on-one direction or group fellowship and discernment. Suffering, contemplation, and the Scriptures share the characteristic of being discerned best within the Christian community. There is no room for a Lone Ranger attitude in the face of these mysteries.

RESOURCES FOR FURTHER STUDY

The apophatic and kataphatic traditions, as revealed by their most famous proponents, St. John of the Cross and the anonymous author of *The Cloud of Unknowing* (apophatic), and St. Ignatius of Loyola and St. Teresa of Avila (kataphatic), are presented in a balanced and insightful fashion in Harvey D. Egan, S.J.'s *Christian Mysticism*, published by Pueblo Publishing Company. Fr. Egan also discusses the spirituality of two modern contemplatives, Teilhard de Chardin and Thomas Merton.

Meditation in the modern oriental sense of the word is a common way of inducing the apophatic experience. Centering prayer is a Christian method of meditation designed to help Christians empty themselves and experience God's fullness. Developed by Cistercian monks, Basil Pennington, Thomas Keating, and William Menninger from the guidelines proposed in *The Cloud of Unknowing*, centering prayer has been widely embraced as a practical tool for invoking contemplative prayer.

The spiritual exercises of St. Ignatius are quite valuable for sparking kataphatic contemplation. A very readable and practical application of the wisdom of St. Ignatius can be found in the series of books on prayer by Thomas Green, S.J., published by Ave Maria Press. Fr. Green blends the Ignatian tradition masterfully with insights from St. John of the Cross, St. Teresa of Avila, and the author of the *Cloud of Unknowing*.

An excellent and very popular Christian personal growth resource which incorporates both contemplative streams are the books and tapes of Anthony de Mello, S.J. A listing of his works can be found in the appendix.

SYNTHESIS

Apophatic and kataphatic contemplation are not mutually exclusive or independent streams of spirituality, but different aspects of the same journey towards God, which goes by way of the cross and resurrection. A person, stimulus, or event cannot be classified as solely amenable to either kataphatic or apophatic contemplation. Ideally the two should be integrated according to the will of God as revealed in life circumstances and amid our sincere efforts.

Our experience of these complementary paths of the contemplative life[102] parallels human existence in that it is normally cyclical. We have good days and bad days, joyful periods and sad ones, times to celebrate and times to mourn. There are times we can discern and praise God in incarnational realities, and times when we find Him in silence and the interior void which only He can fill. Each day is a mysterious mixture of both. Following the example of Job, our challenge is to bring both positive and negative experiences before God, and to ask what He wishes to accomplish in our lives through these events. Without being scrupulous over minor occurrences of which common sense dictates we should simply let go, we can view each day as a contemplative opportunity to see things differently and seek God's will amid both lit and darkened paths.

Job learned that one never knows when and how God will reveal Himself. This is an excellent point to remember when we try to live as active contemplatives. Consider the fleeing Elijah, who found God not in the earthquake or the fire, but in the still, small voice.[103] Abraham encountered God in strangers.[104] It is fitting that we conclude our study of Job with reflections on a complementary passage in Scripture, Mt 25:31-46, which reveals the practical ends to which our contemplative and reconciliatory response to life and suffering should lead.

CHAPTER ELEVEN

Emmanuel: Where Am I When God Needs Me?

Throughout our reflections upon Job, the parallel themes of God's presence and absence have drawn our attention. We have asked, "Where is God when you need Him?", and the book of Job has told us that (despite appearances) He hears our cry and is present to us. While we accept this on faith, sometimes it doesn't seem to be enough. Job's timeless words speak for sufferers everywhere: "If I speak, this pain I have will not be checked; if I leave off, it will not depart from me."[105] God has ordered things such that in times of suffering, prayer alone is not sufficient; we need human comforting as well. It is this reality with which we will close our study. The parable of the Last Judgment from Matthew's Gospel provides us with motivation amid suffering, care-giving, and the humdrum of daily life. It elevates the struggles of Job and his descendants to Christological and eternal proportions. In a mystical sense, this passage completes the story of Job, for it reveals the fruits of true religion and integrity, themes which are central to Job.

If suffering and stress are the signs of the times, as discussed in chapter one, then the Last Judgment parable (Mt 25:31-46) is a passage for the times. It fulfills the description of Hebrews 4:12: "Indeed, the word of God is living and active, sharper than any two-edged sword, piercing until it divides soul from marrow; it is able to judge the thoughts and intentions of the heart."

The Last Judgment scene describes in simple terms how the word of God judges us. Jesus has equated love of neighbor as yourself with love of God, and our eternal future depends on our response to this call. Let us engage in *lectio divina* [106] on this passage, mindful of the themes and morals articulated in Job.

Because we do not experience the stages of meditation, prayer, or contemplation on every passage in distinct fashion, it is not accurate to readily distinguish between these steps in written analysis. Sometimes these distinctions become artificial and mechanical; the experience of prayer is too holistic and interactive to articulate precisely. For example, within the reading phase, meditation or prayer may spontaneously arise. The notes in the *lectio* section may seem to include reflections and applications more appropriately classified as *meditatio*. Likewise with the *oratio* and *contemplatio* sections. In such cases, priority is given to thought flow and clarity at the expense of exact classifications. Further, if a section of the text does not inspire me to prayer and contemplation (though it may for others), I will exclude commenting on the *oratio* or *contemplatio* stages.

LECTIO DIVINA OF MATTHEW 25:31-46

Lectio

"When the Son of Man comes in his glory, and all the angels with him, he will sit on the throne of his glory. All the nations will be gathered before him, and he will separate people one from another as a shepherd separates the sheep from the goats, and he will place the sheep at his right and the goats at the left" (Mt 25:31-33). *(Spoken or whispered slowly and aloud, and repeated)*

- Note the aura of glory and the heavenly pageantry that surrounds the Son of Man's arrival in judgment. This recalls the Joban scene of Yahweh before His heavenly court.[107] In a mystical sense, this judgment scene fulfills the opening scene of Job: We have all undergone our tests, unbeknownst to us, and the transcendent, glorious Lord comes to render judgment.

- The Greek expression for Son of Man could also be translated as "the Man." While it does have apocalyptic precedent in several books of the Hebrew Scriptures, Jesus' usage seems to signify His status as the new Adam, the representative person.

  As Son of Man, Jesus becomes everyman, including partaking in their suffering. He brings to fulfillment the representative suffering of Job. Our response to Him in the person of our neighbor is His criteria for judgment, just as it was for Job's friends. Is our religious disposition self-serving or life-giving? The care-giving vocation of all persons is now revealed.

- The Greek word *ethne*, translated as nations, is the subject of scholarly debate. At issue is the universality of this passage. A sizable minority of scholars conclude that *ethne* refers only to the Gentiles. Christian tradition has generally opted to view the passage as more universal, with nations representing all persons of all times.

- Jesus' and Matthew's audience would have recognized the dramatic, unmistakable nature of this separation; the distinction between sheep and goats would be obvious to first century Palestinians.

- In separating them "one from another," the particularization aspect of this passage is introduced. Each person is considered separately. Seemingly minor details take on great importance.

Lectio

"Then the king will say to those at his right hand, 'Come, you that are blessed by my Father, inherit the kingdom prepared for you from the foundation of the world; for I was hungry and you gave me food, I was thirsty and you gave me something to drink, I was a stranger and you welcomed me, I was naked and you gave me clothing, I was sick and you took care of me, I was in prison and you visited me.' Then the righteous will answer him, 'Lord, when was it that we saw you hungry and gave you food, or thirsty and give you something to drink? And when was it that we saw you a stranger and welcomed you, or naked and gave you clothing? And when did we see you sick or in prison, and visited you?' And the king will answer them, 'Truly, I tell you, just as you did it to one of the least of these who are members of my family, you did it to me.' " (Mt 25:34-40). *(Spoken or whispered slowly and aloud, and repeated)*

- The invitation of the king is amazingly gentle, simple, and succinct. The blessing is not done by humans, as when Job blessed God despite his suffering, but by God. Note that the blessing is of Jesus' Father. This brings to mind Jesus' frequent references to His Father in the Gospel of John, where He proclaims that our response to Him is our response to the Father. This passage takes the connection a step further by giving our response to suffering and deprived persons a Christological and soteriological[108] context. The relating of love of neighbor to love of God is anticipated in Mt 10:40-42 and throughout chapter 18, but most directly in Mt 22:34-40.

- The kingship of Jesus contrasts with that of earthly kings. The king in the Last Judgment parable identifies Himself with the humblest of His subjects. He is less interested in praise (Lord, Lord) than in compassionate faith in action.

- The central theme of this passage, divine justice, expands upon Yahweh's illustrations of His providential presence in chapters 38-41 of Job. Job's desire for a redeemer, an Emmanuel in suffering, is fulfilled by the Son of Man. Note that the saved are described as righteous, thereby recalling Job's status as a just person.

- There are no "as if" clauses in Jesus' identification with the suffering. As Jesus' strong assurance, "Amen, I say to you," reveals, our response to human sufferers *is* our response to Christ. His proclamation of the salvific nature of works of mercy would have surprised neither His Jewish audience nor the Jewish Christians of Matthew's community. That such deeds were deemed performed directly to Christ would have.

- As in Job, questions play an important part in this passage. The righteous cannot recall having encountered and served Jesus, and are surprised at His commendation.

None of their deeds seemed heroic. It is not clear from the text whether they even remembered their acts of charity. Their goodness flowed naturally from basic human compassion. They simply rendered a loving, practical response to an undesirable human situation. We don't know for sure whether religion was their underlying motivation. Their favorable judgment dramatizes the linkage Jesus had made between love of neighbor and love of God.[109]

If this seems to be an overly humanistic interpretation, recognize that it is understood by any Christian sincerely trying to love others that they cannot do so apart from God's help and grace. As St. Paul bemoans in Romans 7:13-25, despite our good intentions, temptation is always at hand when we try to do good. We therefore end up doing the very thing we wished to avoid. Christians who think they can act with compassion apart from their faith in God and His strengthening presence in their heart are self-deluded.

This passage constitutes a severe warning to those who would sharply differentiate love of neighbor and love of God. As the first letter of John asks, how can we claim to love God, whom we have not seen, when we do not love our neighbor, who is right before us?[110] John states this question in language remarkably reminiscent of the Last Judgment scene: "If someone who has worldly means sees a brother in need and refuses him compassion, how can the love of God remain in him? Children, let us love not in word or speech but in deed and truth."[111]

- Another point of scholarly attention is the identity of "these least brothers of mine." The general tendency among Roman Catholic theologians, in accordance with traditional Catholic interpretation, is to regard them as all human sufferers. Protestant scholars seem to lean towards identifying them as Christians or Christian missionaries. This latter interpretation usually coincides with the trans-

lation of *ethne* as Gentiles. Those who opt for the former
interpretation cite the universal setting of the parable and
the priority of the love command in Matthew. Those who
limit "these least brothers of mine" to Christians point to
prior references in Matthew in which Jesus refers to His
followers (and Matthew to Christian missionaries) as "little
ones." Proponents of the former interpretation counter
that the context of Jesus' earlier words is ecclesiastical,
whereas this scene possesses universal dimensions,
thereby precluding a limitation of this phrase to
Christians.

One can synthesize these contrasting interpretations in a
pastoral context by concluding that our response to both
human sufferers and ministers of the Gospel is our response to Christ. The earlier passages in Matthew already
proclaimed that service rendered to followers of Jesus was
service rendered to Him. In light of Jesus' assumption of
the suffering and sins of the whole world onto Himself,
and the unconditional love of God, it is difficult to see how
God would identify Himself exclusively with Christian
missionaries in a passage that speaks of eternal judgment. Jesus is present in all human suffering, regardless of
race, culture, or creed. Could compassion shown to individuals of other faiths be any less important than that
shown to Christians? In matters of love, it is human beings, not God, who are discriminatory.

• The traditional Christian "corporal works of mercy" are
taken from this passage. Note the striking parallel with
chapter 58 of Isaiah.

Meditatio

• The word "inherit" is a key both to this passage and the
Gospel as a whole. Human beings are forever tempted to

use violence to achieve their objectives, whether to amass earthly riches or prevent others from entering the heavenly kingdom.[112] In this passage, the gentle king offers His true subjects a kingdom "prepared from the foundation of the world." They have inadvertently disposed themselves to this gift through the path of meekness and mercy. For Matthew, the Beatitudes are not only the spiritual charter of discipleship, but the criteria of judgment as well. In the Last Judgment scene, the beatitude, "Blessed are the merciful, for they will be shown mercy,"[113] is fulfilled.

Three other beatitudes are of similar relevance: "Blessed are the poor in spirit, for theirs is the kingdom of heaven.[114] "Blessed are they who mourn, for they will be comforted."[115] "Blessed are the meek, for they will inherit the land."[116]

Note the repetitive theme of God generously rewarding humility and compassion. The righteous don't have to grab for their reward; God gladly and freely bestows it on them in His own time. It seems that the righteous don't "earn" their reward, they inherit it. The word inheritance is important because it emphasizes the originator of the gift, our Heavenly Father, and its freely bestowed nature. Nor can it be given to just anyone. One must be worthy of inheritance. In accordance with the thought of the Letter to the Hebrews, Jesus is the first to inherit the Kingdom, and He is not ashamed to call us brothers.[117] In the Last Judgment scene, the brotherly connection between Jesus and human sufferers culminates in the mysterious presence of Christ. Suffering becomes the bridge to our inheritance, just as it was for Jesus. We receive this inheritance through our relationship to Him, who has identified Himself as our brother at other points in the Gospels as well.[118]

• In this passage, we see the fulfillment of Jesus' earlier promises concerning providence: Every hair of our head is counted, and not even a sparrow falls to the earth without our Father noticing. In Mt 25:40, each individual act, done to just one person, has salvific connotations. God overlooks nothing. For God, human sufferers, regardless of their moral quality (e.g., it is not clear whether those in prison are jailed for the Gospel or for a less desirable reason), are Christ's brothers and sisters, in the surprising revelation which determines salvation, they are Christ Himself! The divine standpoint which dominates this passage recalls the theocentric and joyful perspective of the Yahweh Speeches in chapters 38-41 of Job.

Conversely, in humanity's eyes, human suffering appears to have little or no meaning. It is therefore sensible to desensitize ourselves and rationalize away minor injustices, indiscretions, and apathies. From here it is only a short step to perceive things as meaningful only to the extent that they are significant and effective. This attitude manifests itself in cultural, institutional, and personal violence against the defenseless and "useless" in our society.

Jesus' words invite us to reflect on whether we are discriminatory in our compassion, like the friends of Job. Do we take it upon ourselves to judge whether certain individuals are worthy of our compassion? This passage brings to mind the Joban theme, echoed throughout Scripture, of unconditional love. Do we need a reason or reward to love Jesus as we find Him in our neighbor?

• Perhaps the real issue of identity in this passage is not who "these least brothers of mine" are in the Evangelist's and Jesus' mind, but who they are in mine. Do I limit this group to those in situations of extreme poverty or despair, or do I include all persons in this category? Suffering is part of everyone's life, even when this is not readily apparent. Do I include my family, friends, and professional or ministerial associates in this class? Do I include myself, both in terms of vulnerability to others and vulnerability to self? Am I willing to be kind to myself and accepting of my flaws, or do I insist on cross-examining and whipping myself? Do I recognize that when I mercilessly indict myself, I do so to Jesus? Conversely, when I forgive and accept myself, do I realize that I extend these graces to Christ? It can be easier to love those far away than those in our midst, including ourselves. Christian prophets from St. Paul to Mother Teresa have shared these simple but difficult words of wisdom: "Charity begins at home." Once we assimilate this truth, our homes inevitably become larger, and our love more fruitful and practical.

Oratio

Dear Father, I ask Your forgiveness for the many times that I turn You away in the person of my sister and brother in need. I confess my hard-heartedness and lack of generosity. I acknowledge that I sometimes judge whether individuals are worthy of my love. Help me to love You in the person I meet every day.

God, preserve me from pride in the times that I do serve You in my neighbor. Help me to look on Heaven as a gift and reward that flows from Your kindness and fidelity, rather than something I have earned. Help me to avoid using this passage as a call to hyperactivity: I might be tempted to use kindness to persons and causes as a means for getting in good with You, and therefore miss the whole purpose of compassion. Help me to focus on the person, rather than my anticipated reward.

As I await in hope my eternal reward, help me get through these difficult times on earth. Reaching out to others requires sacrifice on my part; I often recoil and rebel at this. I want to give without hurting, yet this is not always possible. Help me to persevere and to truly repent and seek forgiveness for the times I close my heart to You and my neighbor. I ask this through Christ, our Lord and brother. Amen.

Contemplatio

My outlook on life would be radically different if I believed that I met Christ in every human encounter. I would be much more courteous and respectful of others. I would be more generous and compassionate with my time. I wouldn't want to miss either Jesus or my neighbor because I was in a hurry.

God, I place myself in silence before You. Of myself, I fail to respond with love to those in need. I come up with a thousand good reasons why I cannot help them, even in little ways. I would only help when it was convenient for me, when I got something out of it, or if it didn't require me to suffer as well.

Only through Your grace can I become aware of both the hidden and obvious needs of others. Only with Your help can I persevere in reaching out to others. I need to gain strength from You in order to withstand the temptation to place myself before others. I need your Holy Spirit to help me recognize when and how I can serve You in my neighbor.

I sit now in silence, and ask You to grant me discernment, love, and courage. Awaken me to Your presence in the person of the human sufferer, including myself. Help me develop self-esteem and respect for others based on Your presence in us as broken persons made in Your image. I desire to be gentler and less judgmental of both my neighbor and myself. Help me to be creative, generous, patient, and gentle with the suffering and brokenness in my neighbor *and* in myself.

Lectio

"Then he will say to those at his left hand, 'You that are accursed, depart from me into the eternal fire prepared for the devil and his angels; for I was hungry and you gave me no food, I was thirsty and you gave me nothing to drink, I was a stranger and you did not welcome me, naked and you did not give me clothing, sick and in prison, and you did not visit me.' Then they also will answer, 'Lord, when was it that we saw you hungry or thirsty or a stranger or naked or sick or in prison, and did not take care of you?' Then he will answer them, 'Truly, I tell you, just as you did not do it to one of the least of these, you did not do to me.' And these will go away into eternal punishment, but the righteous into eternal life" (Mt 25:41-46). *(Spoken or whispered slowly and aloud, and repeated)*

- The accursed state of those who reject the human sufferer sharply contrasts with the blessing and abundance bestowed by the Father on the righteous. Both paradise and eternal punishment are described as rewards prepared since the foundation of the world.[119]

- The accursed, like the righteous, are surprised that they have encountered Christ on earth. Neither the righteous nor the accursed perceived the hidden reality behind daily events.

- Both the righteous and the accursed call the king "Lord." Their contrast in fates is due to differences in attitude and action, rather than creed. This recalls Jesus' prior warning: "Beware of false prophets, who come to you in sheep's clothing, but inwardly are ravenous wolves. You will know them by their fruits. . . . Not everyone who says to me,

'Lord, Lord,' will enter the kingdom of heaven, but only the one who does the will of my Father in heaven. On that day many will say to me , 'Lord, Lord, did we not prophesy in your name? Did we not drive out demons in your name, and do many deeds of power in your name?' Then I will declare to them, 'I never knew you; Depart from me, you evildoers.' "[120]

Note the similarities in imagery between these passages: wolves in sheep's clothing (paralleling the goats in the Last Judgment scene), the expression "Lord, Lord" (paralleling the "Lord" address in the Last Judgment), Jesus' disavowal of knowing them (in the Last Judgment, the accursed didn't know Christ in the person of the sufferer), and Jesus' command in both passages to "depart from me."

- The passage ends on a positive note with the righteous moving to eternal life.

Meditatio

- This passage could easily inspire a retributive, judgmental attitude. We could look at those who seem to resemble the accursed and pronounce judgment on them. Yet, if we are objective we will see ourselves in the unjust, just as we do in the righteous. We have no justification for judging others when we are guilty of the same. Sometimes we minister to Christ, other times we don't. Only the Lord can discern our fundamental disposition; He alone knows the human heart. He knows why we do and don't serve the sufferer. He is the judge in this passage, not us as individuals or as Church. Those who wish to burn the weeds which clutter the fields had better defer to the divine sower and judge.[121]

- This passage can put a healthy humility in devout religious persons. There is always the danger of looking down on those who do not worship or practice religion as we do. Yet, we may ignore the suffering persons with whom we rub elbows, while these "unorthodox" individuals act with compassion.

Oratio

Father, the retribution aspect of this passage scares me. I do not normally picture you sending people to eternal fires. I get intimidated and fearful when I think of Your justice, because I am aware of all the ways that I do not follow Your will. I do not want to resent or fear You. Teach me how to respect, love, know, and trust You. Grant me the humility to acknowledge my complete dependence on Your saving love.

Contemplatio

Lord, when I am ready to judge other people, and I beseech You to call down fire from heaven upon them,[122] this passage comes to mind. When I sit quietly before You, and contemplate its dramatic message, my desire for retaliation declines. What a horrible future for the wicked! Even if someone seems to profit by their evil on earth, do they really get away with anything?

Only through Your love can I let go of my retributive and vindictive attitude. Liberate me from the sinister delight I feel at the thought of the punishment of my enemies and oppressors. In silence I await You, hoping You will cleanse me of my harshness and complacency.

Lord, slow me down, and gently humble me. May I let You be judge. I will try to resign responsibility for the

human race. Help me to merge my will with Yours, that I
might join You in desiring the repentance and salvation of
all persons, including those who have offended and continue to offend me. Through Jesus, the Lord and King,
Amen.

THE LAST JUDGMENT AND THE
CROSS OF HUMANITY

In our exploration of Job, we have frequently con-
trasted the Christian and secular perspectives on such issues
as suffering, happiness, and personal growth. In this passage of Matthew, which in our *lectio divina* we discovered had
several parallels with Job, the Christian vision of life comes
to full flower.

Many people refuse to believe in God because of the
inexplicable injustices in the world. They have difficulty
reconciling a good God with such unbridled evil and
senselessness. Christians have their moments when they
experience the same inner turmoil. The Last Judgment
passage speaks directly to this dilemma. When we suffer,
Jesus suffers. He is Emmanuel, God with us. This has been a
recurrent theme of Matthew's Gospel,[123] and it will culmi-
nate in the suffering and death of Christ.

Believing that God has gone before and remains with us
in our pain is ultimately a matter of faith and decision. When
we suffer, the belief itself may not comfort us, just as the
reassuring, pious words of Job's friends failed to comfort
him. The challenge of Jesus is remarkably similar to the
challenge of Job: Will we hold on to our integrity and
compassion even when it seems "for nothing"?

The Gospel calls for a decision from the heart, either
for or against Jesus. It openly proclaims that God's will,

which can be a cross for us, must be taken up daily. We can either complain about suffering or try to cooperate with God in bringing something good out of it. As the king in the parable reveals, our deeds need not be heroic or spectacular. Even if we can only help one person in one small way, the deed is significant in God's eyes. We can be sure that if we were that person, we would consider the deed significant. Our daily experiences present equally important extraordinary and ordinary opportunities to share in the crosses of others while sharing our cross as well.

Christianity is not a numbers game where goodness is measured by pragmatic consequences. If we wish to find ways to minister to the suffering parts of others and ourselves, even in seemingly inconsequential circumstances, we will likely discover more than we thought possible. Naturally, the circumstances and requirements may not always be obvious and pleasant. There is no shortage of ambiguity and suffering in our world.

THE SACRAMENT OF THE PRESENT MOMENT

If we knew that Jesus was coming for a personal visit, we would undoubtedly put our best foot forward. However, as the parables immediately preceding the Last Judgment scene warn us, we know neither the day nor the hour. We should always try to be prepared and on our best behavior. Evidently, Jesus prefers surprise visits.

At first, Jesus' unpredictability might be disconcerting, especially if we perceive Him as a judge ready to condemn us. Yet, the New Testament continually reminds us that Jesus came to save, rather than condemn, so we can be assured that our negative prejudice is misguided. Once we get beyond our fear, we discover something very motivational about everyday existence. Every human situation is an opportunity to meet the Lord. Although I may not recognize Him, He is there. I don't have to do anything spectacular to please Him. He appreciates even a small cup of cold water.[124]

Although it is good to be discerning of my motivation for doing good, this awareness should be neither scrupulous nor obsessive. Whereas much of modern psychology seems preoccupied with motives, Jesus is much more practical. He seems less concerned with why we love than how we love. He can teach us how to love unconditionally if we are willing to learn on His terms. We'll never learn anything if we don't make a start. Jesus never refuses our offer of love, no matter how immature or impure. Would a thirsty person refuse a cup of water because our motives were mixed?

Just as no one can heal in Jesus' name and at the same time speak ill of Him,[125] neither can we comfort one in suffering and at the same time tear them down. Note that the Markan passage just referred to also speaks of the reward in store for those who give a cup of cold water to the apostles because they belong to Christ. The practical deeds of kindness extolled by Christ are prefaced by "Amen, I say to you," just as in the Last Judgment scene. At the risk of oversimplifying a complex issue, or of underselling the ideal of pure motives, we can summarize the biblical perspective on charity as follows: "Don't just talk, think, or worry about doing good. You know what to do. Just do it!" We can use imperfect motives or circumstances as an excuse for not doing anything, even the small task at hand, to help our neighbor.

The omnipresence of Jesus is the essence of the "Sacrament of the Present Moment" approach to life. His presence and will in every situation give each moment, however humble and seemingly unimportant, a dignity beyond our ability to comprehend. This inspirational and motivational concept can help us relieve the humdrum of daily existence by looking at life from a "big picture" faith perspective.

HEALING OF SELF THROUGH COMMUNITY AND COMPASSION FOR OTHERS

It is interesting that one of the common denominators in the lives of people who successfully rebound from tragedy is that they discover something to keep them going, some goal or activity that gives meaning to their lives. Very often it involves helping someone who is worse off than they are. Some of the most effective and compassionate caregivers are those who have had or are currently experiencing a similar type of difficulty as the sufferer. The phenomenon of the wounded healer frequently arises in health-care facilities where patients find a common bond and language for sharing their pain and going about the process of holistic healing.

The wounded healer is an excellent example of the principle of redemptive suffering in action. Not only does charity bring eternal rewards, but it can be therapeutic for both giver and receiver in this life as well.

WHEN I AM THE LEAST OF THESE

There are times when there is little we can do for others, and we must instead learn how to be served. This is naturally quite difficult, but the Last Judgment scene offers much needed encouragement. It enables us to discover and fulfill God's will amid our suffering by learning compassion and respect for ourselves and others. We can continue to grieve and dislike our suffering, while treating ourselves as dignified persons. We can pray and visualize the Last Judgment scene as a reminder that our attitude towards ourselves is our attitude towards Christ. How conducive this is to healthy self-esteem! If Christ thinks enough of me to identify Himself with me, even in the worst of situations, then I must be alright and my circumstances redeemable!

Both Job and Matthew insist on unconditional love as constitutive of authentic religious observance. In the Last Judgment scene, Jesus has lifted the second commandment to a Christological plane: When we love our neighbor as ourselves, especially during times of suffering, we love the Son of Man, who became our brother in order to save us. The fact that we can give Jesus such a beautiful gift may be the only thing that inspires and gives us hope during difficult times. Whether we are suffering, care-giving, or both, it is psycho-spiritually healthy and religiously orthodox to lift our thoughts onto the Christological plane and experience the new perspective on life that a theocentric, Emmanuel-conscious outlook can give. For the Jewish believers of Job's time, the suffering Christians of St. Matthew's community, and believers of all ages, the experience of prayer and faith that God is with us (Emmanuel) gives hope and enthusiasm to our efforts to hold on to our faith and integrity amid suffering. For Christians, can any secular personal growth concept or philosophy compare with the Emmanuel life vision in motivational thrust, theological depth, anthropological vision, and staying power? If meeting God can't motivate us, what is the value of those things that can?

For an even more eloquent exhortation to persevere, read the Letter to the Hebrews. Hebrews 10:19-12:13 is a remarkably motivational passage suitable for both personal affirmations and visualization. Hebrews 12:1-2 actually exhorts us to visualize both the great cloud of witnesses and Jesus, the perfecter of our faith, as inspiration for coping with our trials. The following excerpts give some flavor of its kinship to Job: "It was fitting that God, for whom and through whom all things exist, in bringing many children to glory, should make the pioneer of their salvation perfect through suffering."[126] "Because he himself was tested by what he suffered, he is able to help those who are being tested."[127] Note the themes shared in common with Job: Bringing believers to glory, making perfect through suffering, intercession, and the aspect of suffering as a test. Hebrews also reveals suffering as the reason Jesus can identify Himself as humanity's brother, as in the Last Judgment.[128]

TAX COLLECTORS, PROSTITUTES, SINNERS, AND I

At the heart of the Gospel message is the ministry of Christ to the forgotten of society. It is not surprising that all persons, including those who believe in Him, will be judged by their willingness to participate in the Master's mission. Jesus as judge asks only whether we are truly of His flock. Is our perspective and mission in life compatible with His? Is religion our motivation to embrace or avoid the outcasts of society? To answer this question, we must go a bit deeper into the parable.

There are three groups of persons in the Last Judgment scene: the righteous, sufferers, and the accursed. As mentioned in our *lectio divina* reflections, at various times we belong in each of these three groups. It is therefore prudent to incorporate this into our self-understanding and self-image. We must recognize that we are equally capable of being just, unjust, and deprived. If we acknowledge our potential to be unjust, and remain aware of it on a daily basis, we will be less likely to judge others and project our weaknesses upon them. We will be more conscious of and disposed to our need for healing by both God and human healers. It will be much easier to visit individuals in prison and feed the hungry if we recognize that the individual we minister to could just as easily be us. When we encounter such persons, we can appropriate the expression attributed to St. Francis of Assisi: "There but for the grace of God go I."

JOB AND THE LAST JUDGMENT

Job's final speech in chapters 29-31 is a dramatic comparison of his past and present life situation. Among the more prominent aspects of his virtue is his performance of the corporal works of mercy articulated in the Last Judgment scene.[129] These shared values testify that the nature of integrity and compassion is essentially the same in both the Hebrew and Christian Scriptures. God's message all along has been that which the prophet Micah has summarized so well: "With what shall I come before the LORD, and bow myself before God most high? Shall I come before him with burnt offerings, with calves a year old? Will the LORD be pleased with thousands of rams, with ten thousands of rivers of oil? Shall I give my first-born for my transgression, the fruit of my body for the sin of my soul? He has told you, O mortal, what is good; and what does the LORD require of you but to do justice and to love kindness, and to walk humbly with your God."[130]

EMMANUEL AND HUMAN POTENTIAL

I am continually in admiration of Mother Teresa, her order the Missionaries of Charity, and similar individuals and communities. If we are serious about human potential or vocation, we should start by observing these people. If you want to learn about motivation, listen to Mother Teresa. She is straightforward, knows what she wants from herself, others, and the situation, and works hard to accomplish her goals. The "X" factor seems to be her simplicity, her faithfulness to God's will, and her trust in providence. She is persistent and willing to overcome obstacles to fulfill what she perceives as the Lord's will and call. She is respectful of the fact that her cause is not always the cause of others. She is a master of taking things one at a time, and living in the present. Her writings and comments are spiritual, down-to-earth, and occasionally humorous as well. At times she finds Jesus to be demanding and exhausting in His love, as we all do. It is not always easy for her to smile at Jesus or at His brothers and sisters. Yet, with limited resources and amid frequently uncooperative circumstances and persons, she seems to accomplish so much.

When I interact either personally or professionally with individuals dedicated to serving God in others, I am frequently impressed by their human effectiveness as well as their personal warmth. They take the time to really be with people, even at inopportune times, yet seem to achieve more in the long run and for the common good than those who treat others as instruments or obstacles to achieving what they desire.

THE LAST JUDGMENT IN CONTEXT

Before concluding our review of the Last Judgment, it is necessary to acknowledge that we can become moralistic and rigid about this passage, just as we can with any scriptural text. We could posit that serving God in our neighbor is all that is necessary, and that prayer, communal worship, chastity, fasting, etc. are all secondary. Actions and deeds are everything, we say, and even quote Scripture to prove our point. Never mind that we waste time, energy, and opportunities when we reject asceticism and self-discipline in favor of charity, as if they were mutually exclusive. Of course, when we find ourselves exhausted and failing miserably in our subtly pride-driven and egocentric efforts to love others, these complementary practices suddenly become much more essential. Sometimes we learn the hard way that the Christian life is a whole, and that we need to keep the various challenges of Scripture in a healthy tension with each other. What Matthew says must be balanced by the message of John, Mark, Luke, Paul, and Peter, without ignoring the wisdom of the Hebrew Scriptures. The most practical outgrowth of this holistic and unitive approach to Scripture is that we stop judging others and ourselves. When we realize that even our best efforts to comprehend and live the Gospel fall short, we slow down, let God help, stop being so critical, and begin to enjoy the ride more.

Having said the above, it is clear that the Last Judgment is quite harmonious with the rest of Scripture. Its message is strikingly similar to Luke's Good Samaritan parable, which came in response to a question about eternal life and the greatest commandment. The new commandment given by Jesus in His farewell discourse in John's Gospel echoes the message of the aforementioned parables in Matthew and

Luke: Love one another. In passages such as James 2:14-17, St. James echoes Matthew's emphasis on practical acts of compassion. St. Paul's hymn about love in 1 Corinthians 13 is certainly on the same page as St. Matthew.

Given the unique objectives and historical context of each of its books, we cannot expect all of Scripture to merge smoothly. God speaks to individuals and communities in different ways based on their needs and His will. We must keep Matthew's emphasis on faith acted out in word and deed in tension with Luke's emphasis on prayer and compassion, Mark's theme of the cross, and John's exhortation to intimacy with Jesus through faith. Otherwise, we will make the Word of God serve us, rather than vice-versa.

One of the most powerful and practical essays I have read on suffering is that of Pope John Paul II in his encyclical *Salvifici Doloris* (On the Christian Meaning of Human Suffering). Pope John Paul deals with Job, the Good Samaritan parable, and the Last Judgment scene, as well as beautifully articulating the scriptural basis for the redemptive potential of human suffering. One could certainly use the Pope's text as a basis for *lectio divina*, especially given his thoroughly biblical approach.

The Pope's synthesis of the meaning of the Last Judgment scene and the mystery of human suffering is a fitting way to end our story: "The first and second parts of Christ's words about the Final Judgment unambiguously show how essential it is, for the eternal life of every individual, to 'stop,' as the Good Samaritan did, at the suffering of one's neighbor, to have 'compassion' for that suffering, and to give some help. In the messianic program of Christ, which is at the same time the program of the kingdom of God, suffering is present in the world in order to release love, in order to give birth to works of love towards neighbor, in order to transform the whole of human civilization into a 'civilization of love.' In this love the salvific meaning of suffering is completely accomplished and reaches its definitive dimension. Christ's words about the Final Judgment enable us to understand this in all the simplicity and clarity of the Gospel.

"These words about love, about actions of love, acts linked with human suffering, enable us once more to discover, at the basis of all human sufferings, the same redemptive suffering of Christ. Christ said: 'You did it to me.' He Himself is the one who in each individual experiences love; He Himself is the one who receives help, when this is given to every suffering person without exception. He Himself is present in this suffering person, since His salvific suffering has been opened once and for all to every human suffering. And all those who suffer have been called once and for all to become sharers 'in Christ's suffering,' just as all have been called to 'complete' with their own suffering 'what is lacking in Christ's afflictions.' At one and the same time Christ has taught man to do good by his suffering and to do good to those who suffer. In this double aspect He has completely revealed the meaning of suffering."[131]

Closing Prayer

Lord, help us to see Christ in those, including ourselves, who suffer. Give us the grace to seek and accept your redemptive will amid our suffering. Forgive us for the times we fail. May we make time for You every day, not only during times of quiet prayer, but when we encounter You face to face in the situations in which You seem least to be Emmanuel. May the beatitude "Happy are they who mourn, for they shall be comforted"[132] be fulfilled in us. Praised be Jesus Christ, now and forever. Amen.

Appendix

CARLO MARIA CARDINAL MARTINI

THE SCHOOL OF THE WORD

IT CAN HARDLY BE DENIED, I think, that the western world is today experiencing a severe crisis of spiritual desolation. It no longer perceives the mystery of God as present in its major institutions and in the symbols that permeate its public life.

This interior aridity threatens everyone; in particular, it stifles Christians, who are unable to give expression in their daily lives to their faith in the living God. Beyond question, therefore, the Church must help the baptized to make the transition from a traditional faith based on habit and derived from the environment to a personal, interior faith based on conviction and capable of resisting the onslaught of secularism and atheism.

This kind of faith, understood as a dynamic process, is fed and deepened by hearing the word of God. From the very beginning of my episcopal ministry in Milan, my travels through the diocese made clear to me the need people have of the revealed word, their desire to join others in praying and listening to God's word, and the real feasibility of this kind of joint effort.

I also found a certain ignorance of Scripture among even the most highly educated. I therefore resolved to respond as best I could to the exhortation issued by Vatican II in its Constitution on Divine Revelation: that all of the faithful should have direct access to the Bible, because *contact* with the word of God brings an unsuspected wealth of life that is offered as a gift to every Christian. I myself have been reading the Scriptures for over forty years, and at every reading I am astonished to find them utterly new; at every reading I experience the jolt to mind and feelings that stirs a sense of human values and puts me in touch with the values of God.

I was convinced, then, that today, more than in times past, the pages of the Bible can deepen faith by awakening a consciousness of mystery, an openness to the infinite, a movement toward God, and an understanding of God's ways in history. I therefore developed a method that would enable the entire people of God to approach the texts of the Bible step by step.

This method I called the "School of the Word" or "School of Bible-Reading for the Masses." I began to use it with young people whom I invited to the cathedral on the first Thursday of each month. For five years in a row the young came by the thousands, and in ever increasing numbers, even from a distance and even from other dioceses. Their presence proved that the time we spent together (about two hours) in silence, listening to the word, and reflecting on the texts fed them interiorly.

This past year I suggested that these young people give what they have learned to other young people by setting up other "Schools of the Word" in various parts of the diocese. I then invited adults to the cathedral, and in particular laymen and laywomen who are involved in the life of the parish. Once again, the response was surprisingly good. I have also attempted during days of spiritual retreat, to teach children to select some passages from the Old and New Testaments and to understand them.

The "School of the Word" has gradually become a privileged tool of my pastoral activity and of my desire to foster, in communal form as it were, a holiness that is truly popular and not limited to an elite — a holiness that ignores class barriers, is developed in the most unexpected settings, and has the power to overcome all worldliness and fear.

What is a "School of the Word"? It is a step-by-step approach to the biblical text according to the ancient method of the Fathers, which in turn recalls the method of the rabbis and is known as *lectio divina* ("the reading of God's word").

In the Hebrew world the Scriptures were taught in the schools in a very simple way that was adapted to the people. At the same time, certain basic pedagogical and philological principles were operative, as well as a careful progression; if these principles and this progression were neglected, the teaching became fruitless and even counterproductive.

Here, briefly, are the *principles* and *method* of the pedagogy at work in *lectio divina*:

a) The *principles* governing the approach of the Christian people to the sacred text are four in number:

First, *the unity of the Scriptures*. In a "School of the Word" the students must be made to realize that while the Bible is made up of many books it nonetheless forms a unity, inasmuch as every page speaks of God's great plan for the salvation of the human race. Everything refers to the paschal mystery. It is the effort to relate the various texts of the Bible to the unifying mystery that makes all of them yield a meaning, even those that at first glance have little to do with this mystery.

SECOND, *the humanness or "existential relevance" of the Scriptures.* The Scriptures speak to human beings; they give expression to the deepest treasures of the human heart, to the restlessness, sufferings, aspirations, desires, and fears that all human beings share. Individuals find themselves in the Bible, for it puts into words what is permanently human; it lends a voice to the human beings of every age as they speak of their hopes and their distresses. Through simple examples the people learn that the reading of Scripture helps them to that understanding of themselves as individuals and as a community, without which they cannot grasp their own unity or their true relationship to others.

THIRD, *the dynamic character of values.* The Bible expresses values that even today are still developing toward the future of humanity. From the viewpoint of the dynamic movement both of morality and of doctrine the Bible contains values that spur us to advance beyond ourselves by giving us a sense that we human beings are people on a journey. The Bible interacts with human life in a constant movement from life to the word of God and from the word of God back to life.

FOURTH, *the Scriptures are a real presence of Jesus.* A "School of the Word" must help people realize that when they read the Scriptures they can enter into a real communion with Jesus. The expression "real communion" may startle because it echoes the language applied to the eucharistic presence, but Vatican II does not hesitate to assert that the risen Christ is present in the Scriptures and that when we read them or listen to them we can experience this presence.

b) The *method* which Christian tradition has developed for *lectio divina* has four steps: reading, meditation, prayer, contemplation. The sequence is the result of theological and anthropological reflection on the way in which believers approach the word of God in order to assimilate it and make it bear fruit in experience and action.

FIRST, *reading.* The people learn to read and reread a passage by underlining and giving prominence to its key elements: the actions, verbs, acting subjects, attitudes and thoughts, settings, motives for acting. A careful study of all these produces a new and surprising understanding of the text because of the many points that are thus brought to light.

SECOND, *meditation.* In this second phase the people reflect on the abiding value of the passage, by trying to pinpoint the central value in it and its specific message in relation to history and context and situation. The students, whose aim is to discover their authentic selves and find God, single out the attitudes that emerge from the passage on which they are meditating: joy, fear, hope, desire, expectation, and so on.

THIRD, *prayer.* The students are gradually drawn to share the deeper religious sentiments that the text produces or suggests in the name of God; the values assimilated in meditation become motives for praise, thanksgiving, intercession, petition, forgiveness, and so on.

FOURTH, *contemplation.* At some point the multiplicity of sentiments, reflections, and prayers are reduced to unity in contemplation of the mystery of Jesus, the Son of God, a mystery that is contained in every page. This is especially true of the Gospels but it is also true in varying degrees of every passage in the Bible.

The aim, then, of the "School of the Word" is to try to read the word of God in such a way that it turns into prayer in us and sheds light on our lives. It is not possible, of course, to reach this goal in a single leap.

In order to stimulate the people to a prayerful listening to God's word, I usually read and reread a passage aloud, then suggest points for meditation, and, after this, remain silent for a while. I then continue by praying on the passage I have read, thereby leading into a very simple form of personal contemplation.

It is most important for the people to see that the reading of God's word should make Christians challenge themselves: In what way are my life, my activity, my apostolate becoming a word of God in the light of the definitive Word that is Jesus Christ, present in the Scriptures? When they do this, the "School of the Word," which aims at bringing faith to bear on daily life, will express its radical power in certain interconnected attitudes. These are:

a) *Discernment*, that is, the ability Christians develop, with the grace of the Holy Spirit, to see in their lives what is or is not in conformity with the Gospel. It is a discernment of what is best, at a given moment in history, for themselves, for others, for the Church.

b) *Decision*, or the choice of what is in conformity with the Gospel in their lives.

c) *Action* which follows upon discernment and decision. Only the kind of Christian acting, doing, and thinking that is guided by the Holy Spirit can truly be called spiritual activity "according to God."

With the help of the "School of the Word" Christians will gradually become capable of recognizing, despite the ambiguities of history, the signs and glorious presence of the risen Lord in the midst of His people and the local community. My own experience with the "School of the Word" convinces me that it is a tool to be used by ordinary people, by any of the faithful who desire to live authentically Christian lives in a secularized world.

Life in this secularized world demands people who are contemplative, alert, critical, and courageous; it demands that from time to time they make new choices of a kind not made before; it demands attentiveness and new emphases to which they can be alerted by listening to God's word and being sensitive to the mysterious action of the Holy Spirit in hearts and in history.

Cardinal Martini, archbishop of Milan, gave conferences to the American bishops gathered at Collegeville, Minnesota in June 1986. The translation of his article was prepared by Matthew J. O'Connell and reproduced in the May 1987 issue (Vol. 61, 3) of *Worship* and is reproduced here with the permission of the publishers.

Bibliography

CHAPTER ONE
Job, Word Of God, And Healing

Kavanaugh, John Francis. *Following Christ in a Consumer Society: The Spirituality of Cultural Resistance.* Maryknoll, NY: Orbis Books, 1981.

St. Francis de Sales. *Introduction to the Devout Life.* Trans. John K. Ryan. Garden City, NY: Image Books, 1972.

Fichter, Joseph H. *Healing Ministries: Conversations on the Spiritual Dimensions of Health Care.* Mahwah, NJ: Paulist Press, 1986.

Briffa, Salvino. *More Than You Imagine.* Staten Island, NY: Alba House, 1989.

L'Heureux, Conrad E. *Life Journey and the Old Testament.* Mahwah, NJ: Paulist Press, 1986.

Wijngaards, John. *Experiencing Jesus.* Notre Dame, IN: Ave Maria Press, 1981.

Ensley, Eddie. *Prayer That Heals Our Emotions.* San Francisco, CA: Harper & Row, 1988.

Linn, Dennis and Linn, Matthew. *Healing Life's Hurts.* Mahwah, NJ: Paulist Press, 1978.

O'Shaughnessy, Mary Michael. *Feelings and Emotions in Christian Living.* Staten Island, NY: Alba House, 1988.

168   WHERE IS GOD WHEN YOU NEED HIM?

Rosage, David E. *What Scripture Says About Healing: A Guide to Scriptural Prayer and Meditation.* Ann Arbor, MI: Servant Books, 1988.

(Audiocassettes)

Vanier, Jean. *Healing Our Brokenness.* Mahwah, NJ: Paulist Press, 1990.

CHAPTER TWO
Lectio Divina: Framework

Hall, Thelma. *Too Deep for Words: Rediscovering Lectio Divina.* Mahwah, NJ: Paulist Press, 1988.
Mork, Wulstan. *The Benedictine Way.* Petersham, MA: St. Bede's Publications, 1987.
Leclercq, Dom Jean. *The Love of Learning and the Desire for God.* New York, NY: Mentor Omega Books, 1962.
Merton, Thomas. *Contemplative Prayer.* Garden City, NY: Image Books, 1971.

CHAPTER THREE
Lectio Divina: Practical Considerations

Popular Guides to Scripture and Spiritual Reading

Murphy, Richard T.A. *Background to the Bible.* Ann Arbor, MI: Servant Books, 1980.
Keegan, Terence J. *Interpreting the Bible: A Popular Introduction to Biblical Hermeneutics.* Mahwah, NJ: Paulist Press, 1985.
Charpentier, Etienne. *How to Read the New Testament.* New York, NY: Crossroad, 1987.

. . . *How to Read the Old Testament.* New York, NY: Crossroad, 1987.

Harrington, Wilfrid. *The New Guide to Reading and Studying the Bible.* Wilmington, DE: Michael Glazier, Inc., 1978.

Martin, George. *Reading Scripture as the Word of God.* Ann Arbor, MI: Servant Books, 1982.

Kohlenberger, John R. *Words about the Word: A Guide to Choosing and Using Your Bible.* Grand Rapids, MI: Zondervan Publishing House, 1987.

Merton, Thomas. *Opening the Bible.* Collegeville, MN: Liturgical Press, 1970.

Lussier, Ernest. *Biblical Prayer.* Collegeville, MN: Liturgical Press, 1977.

Havener, Ivan. *Spiritual Reading of Scripture.* Collegeville, MN: Liturgical Press, 1979.

Muto, Susan Annette. *A Practical Guide to Spiritual Reading.* Denville, NJ: Dimension Books, 1976.

Ramsey, Boniface. *Beginning to Read the Fathers.* Mahwah, NJ: Paulist Press, 1985.

Dupre, Louis, and Wiseman, James A., ed. *Light from Light: An Anthology of Christian Mysticism.* Mahwah, NJ: Paulist Press, 1988.

Doing Lectio Divina

Rosage, David E. *Follow Me.* Ann Arbor, MI: Servant Books, 1982.

. . . *Abide in Me.* Ann Arbor, MI: Servant Books, 1985.

. . . *Rejoice in Me.* Ann Arbor, MI: Servant Books, 1986.

Martini, Carlo M. *Praying with Saint Luke.* Dublin: Veritas, 1987.

. . . *Bread of the Word.* New York, NY: Catholic Book Publishing Company, 1990.

Guardini, Romano. *The Lord*. Chicago, IL: Regnery Gateway, Inc. 1954.

Journal Writing Guides

Simons, George. *Keeping Your Personal Journal*. Mahwah, NJ: Paulist Press, 1978.
Progoff, Ira. *At a Journal Workshop*. New York, NY: Dialogue House Library, 1975.
Santa-Maria, Maria L. *Growth Through Meditation and Journal Writing: A Jungian Perspective on Christian Spirituality*. Mahwah, NJ: Paulist Press, 1983.
Kelsey, Morton T. *Adventure Inward*. Minneapolis, MN: Augsburg Publishing House, 1980.

CHAPTER FOUR

The Story of Job: I Am Job, We Are Job
Scholarly Commentaries

Bergant, Dianne. *Job, Ecclesiastes*. Wilmington, DE: Michael Glazier, Inc., 1982.
Janzen, Gerald J. *Job*. Atlanta, GA: John Knox Press, 1985.
Habel, Norman C. *The Book of Job*. Philadelphia, PA: Westminster Press, 1985.
Gutierrez, Gustavo. *On Job*. Maryknoll, NY: Orbis Books, 1987.
Gordis, Robert. *The Book of God and Man*. Chicago, IL: University of Chicago Press, 1965.
. . . *The Book of Job: Commentary, New Translation, Special Notes*. New York, NY: Jewish Theological Seminary, 1978.
Pope, Marvin H. *Job*. Anchor Bible. Garden City, NY: Doubleday, 1973.

Dhorme, E. *A Commentary on the Book of Job.* London: Thomas Nelson Sons, 1967.

Andersen, Francis I. *Job: An Introduction & Commentary.* Downers Grove, IL: Inter-Varsity Press, 1966.

Popular Level Resources

Guinan, Michael. *Job.* Collegeville, MN: Liturgical Press, 1986.

Mitchell, Stephen. *The Book of Job.* San Francisco, CA: North Point Press, 1987.

Wiesel, Elie. *Messengers of God: Biblical Portraits & Legends.* New York, NY: Random House, 1976.

Smith, Alfred J., Sr. *Making Sense of Suffering.* Progressive National Baptist Convention.

CHAPTER FIVE
The Morals of the Story

Wolff, Pierre. *Is God Deaf?* Waldwick, NJ: Arena Lettres, 1984.

Suenens, Leon-Joseph. *Nature & Grace.* Ann Arbor, MI: Servant Books, 1986.

Kelsey, Morton. *Christianity as Psychology.* Minneapolis, MN: Augsburg Publishing House, 1986.

Vitz, Paul C. *Psychology as Religion: The Cult of Self-Worship.* Grand Rapids, MI: William B. Eerdmans Publishing Co., 1977.

Michael, Chester and Norrisey, Marie. *Arise: A Christian Psychology of Love.* Charlottesville, VA: The Open Door, Inc., 1981.

Buber, Martin. *I and Thou.* New York, NY: Scribner, 1958.

Lauer, Eugene, and Mlecko, Joel, ed. *A Christian Understanding of the Human Person: Basic Readings.* Mahwah, NJ: Paulist Press, 1982.

Powell, John. *The Christian Vision: The Truth That Sets Us Free.* Allen, TX: Argus Communications, 1984.

. . . *Happiness is an Inside Job.* Allen, TX: Tabor Publishing, 1989.

de Caussade, J.P. *Self-Abandonment to Divine Providence.* Trans. Algar Thorold. Rockford, IL: TAN Books and Publishers, Inc., 1987.

Muggeridge, Kitty. *The Sacrament of the Present Moment.* New York, NY: Harper & Row, 1982.

CHAPTER SIX
Job's Happy Ending

Donnelly, Doris. *Putting Forgiveness into Practice.* Allen, TX: Argus Communications, 1982.

Furey, Robert J. *So I'm Not Perfect.* Staten Island, NY: Alba House, 1986.

CHAPTER SEVEN
The Lord Takes Away

Johnson, Luke Timothy. *Some Hard Blessings.* Allen, TX: Argus Communications, 1981.

St. Gregory of Nyssa. *The Lord's Prayer, The Beatitudes.* Ancient Christian Writers, no. 18. Trans. Hilda C. Graef. Mahwah, NJ: Paulist Press, 1954.

Ciszek, Walter J. *With God in Russia.* Garden City, NY: Image Books, 1966.

. . . *He Leadeth Me.* Garden City, NY: Image Books, 1973.

Walsh, James and Walsh, P.G. *Divine Providence & Human Suffering.* Wilmington, DE: Michael Glazier, Inc., 1985.

Whitney, Barry L. *What Are They Saying About God and Evil?* Mahwah, NJ: Paulist Press, 1989.

Kreeft, Peter. *Making Sense Out of Suffering.* Ann Arbor, MI: Servant Books, 1986.

Wolff, Pierre. *May I Hate God?* Mahwah, NJ: Paulist Press, 1979.

McCloskey, Pat. *When You Are Angry With God.* Mahwah, NJ: Paulist Press, 1987.

Lewis, C.S. *A Grief Observed.* New York, NY: Bantam Books, 1976.

Carretto, Carlo. *Why, O Lord?* Maryknoll, NY: Orbis Books, 1987.

(Audiocassettes)

Stuhlmueller, Carroll. *Suffering and the Biblical Experience of a Compassionate God.* Canfield, OH: Alba House Communications, 1989.

Rohr, Richard. *Job and the Mystery of Suffering.* Kansas City, MO: Credence Cassettes, 1988.

CHAPTER EIGHT
The Lord Gives

Browning, William. *God Really Loves Us.* Collegeville, MN: The Liturgical Press, 1979.

Jamart, Francois. *Complete Spiritual Doctrine of St. Therese of Lisieux.* Staten Island, NY: Alba House, 1961.

CHAPTER NINE
New Testament Models

Martini, Carlo M. *Women and Reconciliation*. Dublin: Veritas, 1987.

. . . *Women in the Gospels*. New York, NY: Crossroad, 1990.

. . . *The Testimony of St. Paul*. New York, NY: Crossroad, 1989.

LaVerdiere, Eugene. *When We Pray . . . : Meditation on the Lord's Prayer*. Notre Dame, IN: Ave Maria Press, 1983.

Crosby, Michael H. *Thy Will Be Done: Praying the Our Father as Subversive Activity*. Maryknoll, NY: Orbis Books, 1977.

Brown, Raymond E. *New Testament Essays*. Garden City, NY: Image Books, 1965.

Lohmeyer, Ernst. *Our Father*. Trans. John Bowden. New York, NY: Harper & Row, 1965.

Lustiger, Jean-Marie. *The Lord's Prayer*. Trans. Rebecca Howell Balinski. Huntington, IN: Our Sunday Visitor, 1988.

CHAPTER TEN
Job: Model of Everyday Mysticism

Egan, Harvey D. *What Are They Saying About Mysticism?* Mahwah, NJ: Paulist Press, 1982.

. . . *Christian Mysticism: The Future of a Tradition*. New York, NY: Pueblo Publishing Company, 1984.

Burrows, Ruth. *Guidelines for Mystical Prayer*. Denville, NJ: Dimension Books, 1976.

Zanzig, Thomas. *Learning to Meditate*. Winona, MN: Saint Mary's Press, 1990.

Keating, Thomas. *Open Mind, Open Heart.* New York, NY: Amity House, 1986.

Keating, Thomas, Pennington, M. Basil and Clarke, Thomas E. *Finding Grace at the Center.* Petersham, MA: St. Bede's Publications, 1978.

Pennington, M. Basil. *Centered Living: The Way of Centering Prayer.* Garden City, NY: Doubleday & Co., Inc., 1986.
. . . *In Search of True Wisdom.* Staten Island, NY: Alba House, 1991.

Schmidt, Joseph F. *Praying Our Experiences.* Winona, MN: Saint Mary's Press, 1980.

Michael, Chester and Norrisey, Marie. *Prayer and Temperament.* Charlottesville, NC: The Open Door, Inc., 1984.

van Zeller, Hubert. *Prayer and the Will of God.* Springfield, IL: Templegate Publishers, 1978.

Dubay, Thomas. *Fire Within: St. Teresa of Avila, St. John of the Cross, and the Gospel — On Prayer.* San Francisco, CA: Ignatius Press, 1989.

Green, Thomas. *Opening to God.* Notre Dame, IN: Ave Maria Press, 1987.
. . . *When the Well Runs Dry.* Notre Dame, IN: Ave Maria Press, 1979.
. . . *Darkness in the Marketplace.* Notre Dame, IN: Ave Maria Press, 1981.
. . .*Weeds Among the Wheat.* Notre Dame, IN: Ave Maria Press, 1984.
. . . *A Vacation with the Lord.* Notre Dame, IN: Ave Maria Press, 1986.

de Mello, Anthony. *Wellsprings.* New York, NY: Image Books, 1986.
. . . *One Minute Wisdom.* New York, NY: Image Books, 1988.
. . . *Sadhana: A Way to God.* New York, NY: Image Books, 1984.

. . . *The Song of the Bird.* New York, NY: Image Books, 1984.
. . . *Heart of the Enlightened.* New York, NY: Image Books, 1989.
. . . *Taking Flight: A Book of Story-Meditations.* New York, NY: Doubleday, 1988.
Valles, Carlos G. *Mastering Sadhana: On Retreat with Anthony de Mello.* New York, NY: Image Books, 1987.

(Videocassettes)

de Mello, Anthony. *A Way to God for Today.* Allen, TX: Tabor Publishing, 1986.
. . . *Wake Up! Spirituality for Today.* Allen, TX: Tabor Publishing, 1987.

(Audiocassettes)

de Mello, Anthony. *Sadhana: A Way to God.* St. Louis, MO: We and God Spirituality Center, 1984.
. . . *Wellsprings.* St. Louis, MO: We and God Spirituality Center, 1986.
. . . *Wake Up to Life.* St. Louis, MO: We and God Spirituality Center, 1989.
. . .*De Mello Satellite Retreat.* St. Louis, MO: We and God Spirituality Center, 1989.

CHAPTER ELEVEN
Emmanuel: Where Am I When God Needs Me?

Vanier, Jean. *Be Not Afraid.* Mahwah, NJ: Paulist Press, 1975.

Martini, Carlo M. *Through Moses to Jesus: The Way of the Paschal Mystery.* Notre Dame, IN: Ave Maria Press, 1988.

Kelsey, Morton T. *Caring: How Can We Love One Another?* Mahwah, NJ: Paulist Press, 1981.

Mother Teresa. *Words to Love By . . .* Notre Dame, IN: Ave Maria Press, 1983.

Le Joly, Edward. *Mother Teresa of Calcutta: A Biography.* New York, NY: Harper & Row, 1983.

Spink, Kathryn. *I Need Souls Like You: Sharing in the Work of Mother Teresa Through Prayer and Suffering.* New York, NY: Harper & Row, 1984.

Lubich, Chiara. *When Did We See You, Lord?* New York, NY: New City Press, 1979.

Montague, George T. *Companion God: A Cross-Cultural Commentary on the Gospel of Matthew.* Mahwah, NJ: Paulist Press, 1989.

"Job Therapy" Workshops

Karl Schultz *offers workshops and retreats on care-giving and therapeutic applications of Job. "Job Therapy: Timeless Model of Holistic Patient Care" is part of the "Building Up the Human" program for personal and professional development. Further information may be obtained by contacting Genesis Personal Development Center at (412) 486-6087, or P.O. Box 201, Glenshaw, Pennsylvania, 15116.*

Endnotes

1 Cf. Hab 1:2.
2 Cf. Lk 22:38.
3 For an explanation of the "for nothing" nature of Job's sufferings, consult chapters four and five, respectively entitled *The Story of Job* and *The Morals of the Story.* "For nothing" is a translation of the Hebrew word *hinnam* which appears in Job in verses 1:9 and 2:3.
4 Cf. Is 55:10-11.
5 Cf. Lk 5:1-11.
6 Latin for divine reading or listening.
7 e.g., the writings of the Saints and Church Fathers (Tradition), as well as quality contemporary spiritual literature (living Church).
8 Cf. Lk 15; Mt 9:13.
9 Refer to the "School of the Word" article by Cardinal Martini in the appendix.
10 Which we can determine by prayer, trial and error, and perhaps counsel with a priest, minister, or spiritual director.
11 Refer to *Self Abandonment to Divine Providence*, published by Tan Books.
12 Cf. Ac 7:60.
13 See chapter 31 of Job for a poetic illustration of his morality.
14 Individuals wishing to pursue the use of a journal for personal growth purposes can consult the writings and workshops of Dr. Ira Progoff, originator of the widely used Progoff Method of journal writing.
15 Cf. *In Ezk* 2.2.1.
16 Cf. Jb 1:9, 2:3.
17 This is not surprising. It is difficult to sell a secular personal growth resource that gives no such guarantees and does not pander to people's wants and dreams.
18 Cf. Heb 5:8-9.
19 As discussed previously, the Sacraments, nature, daily events, and human relationships are also potential opportunities for revelation and contemplation.
20 As previously mentioned, we can use *Lectio divina* with other Christian writings such as that of the Saints, the Early Church Fathers, and respected spiritual writers/directors such as J.P. de Caussade, S.J. While Scripture

should be our primary diet, there may be other works through which God chooses to communicate with us.

21 Currently out of print, but available in most Catholic theological libraries.

22 Cf. Lk 18:1-8.

23 Refer to Cardinal Martini's "School of the Word" article in the appendix.

24 i.e. 587 B.C.

25 i.e. inquiries into the nature of divine justice in light of human suffering.

26 Readers interested in exploring these ancient parallels to Job can consult *The Ancient Near East, Vol. I & II*, edited by James B. Pritchard and published by Princeton University Press. An excellent introduction to the cultural background of Job is contained in *The Book of God and Man: A Study of Job* by Robert Gordis, published by the University of Chicago Press.

27 Curiously, Satan is not specifically named in the Hebrew text as the perpetrator of Job's physical suffering. Perhaps the ambiguity symbolizes the confusion in both our own and Job's mind as to who is ultimately responsible for Job's suffering. Interestingly, in 42:11, the narrator names Yahweh as the source of the suffering inflicted upon Job. To the Hebrew mind, nothing happens outside of God's jurisdiction, even suffering.

28 e.g. Psalm 37.

29 This almost dualistic notion of God was common in the ancient Near East and may be implicit in Job's plea for a heavenly advocate.

30 A revelatory presence of God.

31 The translation of 42:6 is the subject of much debate among scholars. Throughout his speeches, Job uses legal imagery and language in affirming his rights against Yahweh, his presumed prosecutor. One interpretation currently gaining acceptance for the first part of the verse is that Job is simply retracting his lawsuit rather than despising himself. Because the Hebrew verb has no direct object, the translator must supply one.

The traditional rendering of the completion of the verse, that Job repented in dust and ashes, seems contradictory in lieu of Job's innocence and previously defiant lament. For the modern reader repent connotes an affirmation of guilt which is absent from the Hebrew word translated as repent. The solution opted for in Gustavo Gutierrez' work *On Job* (pp. 86-87) seems most compatible with the overall thrust of the book. This rendering suggests that Job changed his mind (a neutral rendering of repent) *about* dust and ashes (i.e. the human condition.)

32 Cf. Jb 1:8, 2:3.

33 Cf. Jb 42:7-9.

34 Cf. Jb 42:7-9.

35 Cf. Jb 40:3-5.

36 For example, cf. Lk 18:1-8, 11:5-13.

37 Cf. Lk 18:1-8.

38 See *I and Thou*, by Martin Buber, published by Scribner Press.

39 Cf. Jb 38:1-39:30.

40 Cf. Jb 40:6-41:26.

41 Although we do not have the same mythology-influenced cosmology as the ancient Semites, there are parts of nature which each of us either fears or finds distasteful.

42 Cf. Jb 40:15.

43 Cf. Jb 42:1-6.

44 Cf. Jb 42:1-6.

45 For example, if I have a particular inclination towards finding God in nature, I may be moved into contemplation by the lush nature imagery of God's response. Perhaps I worry about the chaotic beasts in my own life, such as snakes or other reptiles which give me the creeps. Inspired by God's delight in these creatures, I can begin to see them in a new light.

46 Unlike the modern sufferer, Job never questioned God's power. The Hebrew faith recognized that no one could rival Yahweh. As Job would later state: "I know that you can do all things, and that no purpose of yours can be hindered" (cf. Jb 42:2).

47 The Hebrew word translated as integrity and used to describe Job also implies wholeness.

48 Cf. Jn 9:1-3.

49 Cf. 1 Cor 4:1-5.

50 Cf. Jb 1:21.

51 Cf. Lk 6:37; Mt 7:1.

52 Cf. Jb 42:11.

53 Cf. Gn 3:16.

54 For example, chapter three of Job uses the language of chapter one of Genesis to describe Job's anguish.

55 Cf. Jb 31:13-15 where Job discusses his concern for the dignity of his slaves. Job recognizes that they come from the same Lord as Job does. This perspective was quite progressive for its time, surpassing even the Greek ethicists.

56 Cf. Jb 42:6.

57 As previously discussed, although most translations refer to Job as repenting in dust and ashes, an equally acceptable rendering is that Job changed his mind (the Hebrew word translated as repent does not necessarily imply guilt, as the English equivalent does) about dust and ashes (i.e. the human condition). Note the overtones of the language of Genesis, in particular Abraham's referring to himself as dust and ashes (cf. Gn 18:27).

58 Cf. Rm 8:28.

59 Cf. Jb 1:21.

60 Cf. Jb 2:9.

61 Cf. Jb 1:9, 2:3.

62 The Greek word *teleios* usually translated as perfect also means whole, mature, or complete. It is the Greek equivalent of the Hebrew word *tam* used in the prologue to describe Job as a person of integrity or wholeness.

63 Cf. Mt 5:3-12.
64 Cf. Col 1:24.
65 Cf. Mt 25:31-46.
66 Cf. Mt 13.
67 Cf. Mt 7:1-5; Lk 6:37-38.
68 Cf. Heb 11:6.
69 i.e., Scripture, Church, Tradition, fellowship, legitimate forms of culture — arts, music, literature, etc.
70 Cf. Jm 1:17.
71 Cf. Mt 20:1-16.
72 Cf. Mt 5:45.
73 Cf. Heb 12:1-14.
74 Cf. Mt 4:4.
75 The Greek word rendered as daily, *epiousios*, is uncertain in meaning. Other possibilities are "for the morrow" or "for subsistence," as well as meanings related to the Eucharist. The sense seems to be that which we need or require.
76 Cf. Mt 5:37.
77 i.e., What's in it for me?
78 i.e., with God, self, others, and the material world.
79 Cf. Jb 9:16.
80 Cf. Gn 22:1-19.
81 Cf. Lk 2:35.
82 Cf. Jn 19:25-27.
83 Cf. Lk 2:41-51.
84 Cf. Jn 2:1-11.
85 Latin term for "let it be done to me according to your word" (cf. Lk 1:38).
86 Cf. Mt. 25:40.
87 Cf. Jn 2:1-11.
88 Cf. Lk 1:46-55.
89 Cf. Lk 2:41-51.
90 Cf. Jn 19:25-27.
91 A particularly insightful and readable discussion of the Lord's Prayer is Fr. Eugene La Verdiere's *When We Pray . . .: Meditations on the Lord's Prayer*, published by Ave Maria Press.
92 Cf. *When we pray . . .*, pp. 147-157.
93 Cf. Jb 42:5-6: "I had heard of you by word of mouth, but now my eye has seen you. Therefore I disown what I have said, and repent in dust and ashes."
94 Cf. Rm 1:19-20.
95 Cf. Rm 8:18-23.
96 Cf. Jb 3:23.
97 Cf. Jb 7:17-18, 23:8-9.
98 i.e., while Elihu was pontificating, chapters 32-37 of Job.

99 Cf. Lk 18:1-8.

100 Cf. Mt 15:21-28.

101 Cf. Lk 23:39-43.

102 A contemplative approach to life is evidenced not only in monks and mystics but in all persons who measure and respond to their life experiences in the context of their relationship to God. The contemplative life implies that we think about life in light of God and His decisive intervention in human history, especially the incarnation (the Word made flesh) and the redemption (the paschal mystery).

103 Cf. 1 K 19:9-18.

104 Cf. Gn 18:1-15.

105 Cf. Jb 16:6.

106 For a review of *lectio divina*, refer to chapters two and three of this book. It is also suggested that the reader do their own *lectio divina* on this passage, starting by saying the words slowly aloud and if possible in rhythm with one's breathing. If it seems to take several repetitions before the words begin to sink in, recall the Hebrews text cited above which speaks of the word of God affecting us at the level of soul (or mind), spirit, and body (in this text, joints and marrow). We can't expect such penetration immediately. *Lectio divina* is most fruitful when it flows with the pace of grace.

107 Cf. Jb 1:6-12, 2:1-6.

108 i.e., related to salvation.

109 Cf. Mt 22:34-40.

110 Cf. 1 Jn 4:20.

111 Cf. 1 Jn 3:17-18.

112 Cf. Mt 11:12.

113 Cf. Mt 5:7.

114 Cf. Mt 5:3.

115 Cf. Mt 5:4.

116 Cf. Mt 5:5.

117 Cf. Heb 2:11.

118 Cf. Jn 20:17; Mt 28:10.

119 The damnation statement uses "prepared for the devil and his angels," which we assume represents primordial origins.

120 Cf. Mt 7:15-16a, 7:21-23.

121 Recall the parable of the weeds among the wheat, a story unique to Matthew (cf. Mt 13:24-30, 36-43).

122 Cf. Lk 9:54.

123 Cf. Mt 1:23, 18:20, 28:20.

124 Cf. Mt 10:42.

125 Cf. Mk 9:38-40.

126 Cf. Heb 2:10.

127 Cf. Heb 2:18.

128 Cf. Heb 2:11-12.

129 Cf. Jb 29:12-17, 31:5-32.
130 Cf. Mi 6:6-8.
131 Taken from the conclusion of chapter seven of the Vatican Translation of *Salvifici Doloris.*
132 Cf. Mt 5:4.